ESSENTIAL
Guitar
Chords
THE EASY-TO-USE GUIDE

Joshua Roland

ARCTURUS

ARCTURUS

This edition published in 2010 by Arcturus Publishing Limited
26/27 Bickels Yard, 151–153 Bermondsey Street,
London SE1 3HA

ISBN: 978-1-84837-527-7
AD001365EN

Printed in China

Contents

INTRODUCTION

In 1976, during the height of punk, the British fanzine *Sniffing Glue* published a diagram of three basic chords – E, A and D major – with the caption, 'Here are three chords, now form a band'. It wasn't an idle boast. Simplicity is the key to popular music.

Early rock and roll rarely used more than three chords – just listen to the early hits of Chuck Berry, Little Richard and Elvis and you will hear variations on what is known as the three-chord trick – the tonic, subdominant and dominant major chords (EAB, ADE, CFG etc) used in endless permutation. These early hits should, in theory, have been almost identical because they shared the same musical formula, and yet the best of them were distinctive and exciting because the songwriters and musicians who made them used the chord progressions as a platform from which to soar wherever their muse led them.

The same limitations faced the garage bands of the 1960s and the punks in the mid-1970s, both of whom adhered to the 'back-to-basics' approach and established that key rule of popular music – the fewer number of chords used, the more memorable the song.

This is not to say that sophistication or a more extensive musical vocabulary is bad – far from it – but familiarity with a few dozen chords and a surfeit of enthusiasm can be more valuable and productive than a PhD in harmonic theory. The musical snobbery that permeated the late 1960s and early 1970s, which declared that guitarists were not worthy of the name unless they could play as fast as Eric Clapton or Jimi Hendrix, is clearly bunk and self-defeating. John Lennon wrote one of the most influential songs of the 1960s, 'Tomorrow Never Knows', using only one chord. Not only did it prove to be a highlight of the *Revolver* album, it also initiated the psychedelic era. Clearly, it is not the number of chords that make a song special, nor their harmonic complexity, but what you do with the chords you choose.

There are, in theory, in excess of 2,000 chords, but few popular songs use more than half a dozen. For this book I selected only those chords you need to learn and a few variations so that you can choose to play whichever version you find more comfortable. For example, if you have short fingers you may that find the alternative fingerings placed higher up the fretboard are easier to master. They also have a distinctive, lighter 'voicing', making them ideal to accompany another guitarist playing the fuller versions of the same chord lower down the neck.

The chords are listed by key, so that you can begin by learning C major in its simplest (and most essential) form, as a basic triad, and then familiarize yourself with a useful variation (the first inversion), before moving on to C as a barre chord (all barre chords are essential), then C minor in its most basic form and the same minor as a barre chord. If you are a beginner, you can then stop there and skip to C♯ in its simplest form (note that C♯/D♭, D♯/E♭, F♯/G♭ and A♯/B♭ are in fact the same notes, so both notations are always given). You can ignore the augmented and diminished chords and the more 'advanced' variations such as suspended 2nd, major/minor 7th etc – at least for the time being. But there will come a time when you come across these more harmonically sophisticated chords and realize that a basic C minor is no substitute for a C minor add 9th, if that is what the songwriter used at a key point to produce a specific effect. When you encounter an unfamiliar chord, all you have to do is flip to that page and you will find it laid out clearly in a diagram form which you can refer to as often as you need.

This chord book is designed to get you started on playing your guitar from day one. Whether you want to play songs by your favourite artists or even write your own, this streamlined, user-friendly dictionary will provide you with all the chords you need and more. So don't waste another minute – get started!

HOW TO READ A CHORD DIAGRAM

A guitar neck diagram is the easiest way to learn guitar chords. Take a look at these examples:

C Major

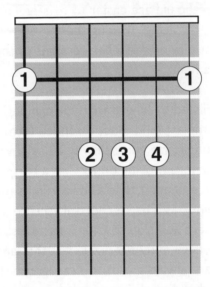

The thin white horizontal border at the top of the box represents the nut at the top of the neck. The strings from left to right are bottom E (thickest), A, D, G, B and top E (thinnest).

The circled figures show which fingers to use, with 'I' indicating the index finger. A bar joining two notes means that you should use that finger to hold down the notes across the strings in between. In the diagram above the index finger of the left hand holds down all six strings at the second fret.

C♯ or D♭ Minor 9th

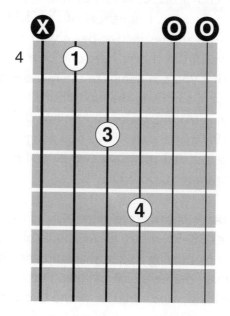

When the nut is not shown this means that the chord is to be played higher up the fretboard. A number outside the diagram at the top left indicates which fret the shape should start on.

A circled 'X' tells you to mute or not to play that string while an 'O' indicates that this should be played as an open string (not fretted).

PLAYING CHORDS

You do not have to be able to read music or understand the theory of harmony to play the guitar. You do not even have to learn scales, although all these skills should be acquired in due course. But if you are impatient to begin playing or even writing your own songs you can do so in a matter of weeks by memorizing the chord shapes in this book and practising simple chord progressions (sequences of chords) until the changes are smooth and instinctive. Begin with a simple progression in which the chords have one or more fingerings in common, so that you can minimize the number of fingers which have to move to create the next chord in the chain. For example, in moving from C major to A minor (a favourite progression in 1950s and early 1960s pop songs) you can take advantage of the fact that there are two pivotal fingers, '1' and '2', which are common to both chords.

There are also barre chords (see page 14) and moveable shapes (see pages 38–51) which allow you to play a sequence of chords simply by moving a fixed shape up and down the fretboard. The main theme or riff of Deep Purple's 'Smoke On The Water' and Hawkwind's 'Master of the Universe' are classic examples of this type of progression.

The key to making chords sound clean is to place the fingers just between the frets and press firmly but not too hard. If you place your fingers too close to the fret you may create fret buzz and if you press too hard or too lightly you may distort the tone so that the chord will sound out of tune. But with practice you will develop an instinctive feel for how much pressure to apply, and if you practise for 30 minutes a day your fingertips will harden within a fortnight, making it easier to hold down the strings. This is less of a problem if you play a nylon-strung acoustic guitar, but many beginners give up simply because of the initial discomfort felt in holding down the strings on a steel-strung guitar (electric or acoustic). If you find that holding down the strings is too difficult then you may need to have the action (the height of the strings from the fretboard) adjusted by a professional.

Why learn more than the basic chords?

The answer to this often-asked question is simple. If you only played the basic major and minor chords which are the building blocks of most western popular music, then the music would tend to sound 'safe' and conventional. Interest in music, as in most art forms, is generated by the use of the unexpected or unconventional. The more 'advanced' chords – such as augmented, suspended, diminished and 'add9' chords – add or subtract notes in the basic chord so that they take on a new quality or character such as expectation, suspense etc. The way we hear chords is subjective, but certain chord types have become associated with specific types of music (jazz, psychedelia, AOR or album-oriented rock, Merseybeat etc). You may need to develop as large a stock of chords as you can master if you intend to play a wide range of songs.

It is not always an option to substitute an awkward or unfamiliar chord for a more basic version as it can alter the character of the song. For example, swapping an E minor for an E minor 6th loses the distinctive psychedelic tinge of the latter chord, which the writer presumably chose for that effect.

Why learn more than one version of a chord?

Again, the answer to this question is simple once you begin to play songs written by other people. You will soon find that you need more than one version of the basic chords to give you an option when changing between shapes that are far apart on the fretboard. For example, being able to play B minor and F♯/G♭ minor as barre chords gives you the option for a fluid change from a basic A minor shape to an E minor shape using the first finger as a barre or a capo to alter the key of these two basic chords. Otherwise you would have to move all your fingers to form the two shapes, which can be awkward and daunting for the beginner. Learning more than one fingering gives you the choice of which shape to play so that you can ensure smooth changes to the next chord.

What is a capo and what is it used for?

Fitting a capo to the neck of the guitar acts like a barre in altering the key of a chord sequence. For example an E minor, A minor, F major progression, with a capo at the first fret, raises the chords to form F minor, B♭ minor and F♯/G♭ major. The capo fitted at the second fret raises these three chords to F♯/G♭ minor, B minor and G major and so on.

The capo has two applications that will prove invaluable to every guitarist. The first is that it enables you to transpose any sequence of chords to another key which may be more comfortable for you to play or to sing in. For example, if a song in A minor is too low for the singer the whole sequence can be raised to B minor by fitting the capo to the second fret and playing the same shapes which now sound a tone higher. But remember that all the chords will be raised by the same degree by the addition of the capo.

The capo is also useful if you find that the original sequence of chords is too awkward to finger in an open string version. By fitting the capo to a higher fret, you may find that the sequence can be played using easier shapes. Song sheets and chord books will sometimes list a flattened (♭) or sharpened (♯) chord which might be difficult for a beginner, but these can be raised or lowered by fitting a capo, although all the other chords in the sequence will also be raised or lowered of course. In many cases this does not create problems with the other chords in the sequence but it will make the 'awkward' chord playable.

Chord
Directory

Cmaj

C Major Triad
(basic version)

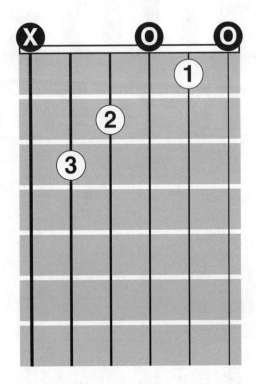

This triad is a simplified version of C major with a lighter sound as the bass note G is missing. Triads are ideal for the beginner, but the fuller C/G version (see next chord) should also be learnt before moving on to barre chords.

If you see the notation C/E in a songbook it simply means play this basic C major triad with the bottom E string open.

C/G

C Major
(second inversion)

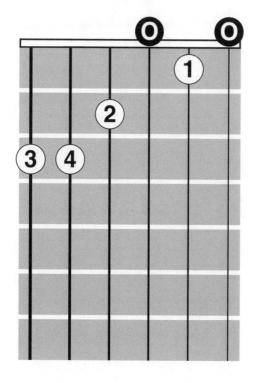

For a fuller sounding C major play this second inversion which adds the low G below the root (add the third finger on the third fret of the bottom E string).

C

C♯/D♭

D

D♯/E♭

E

F

F♯/G♭

G

G♯/A♭

A

A♯/B♭

B

C

C Major
(barre chord)

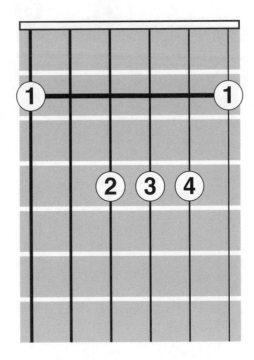

Barre chords can be difficult for the beginner but persistence will pay rewards as each barre shape can create more chords simply by moving the hand up or down the fretboard. Move this chord down to give B♭ major or up to the third fret to make C♯ major. Barre chords appear throughout this chord directory.

Cm

C Minor
(basic version)

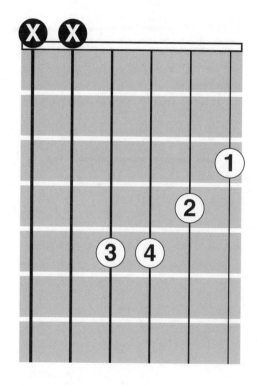

This simplified barre chord places the first finger on the top string only so the bottom two strings cannot be played, but for a fuller-sounding chord the first finger should lie across all six strings at the third fret (see overleaf).

Cm

C Minor
(barre chord)

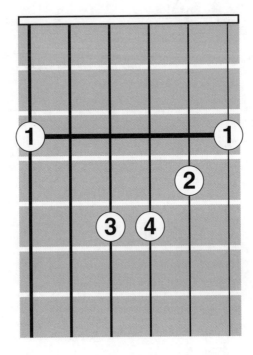

This is the basic A minor triad moved up to the third fret with the first finger acting as a capo to create a barre chord (see page 10 for more about the capo).

C+

C Augmented

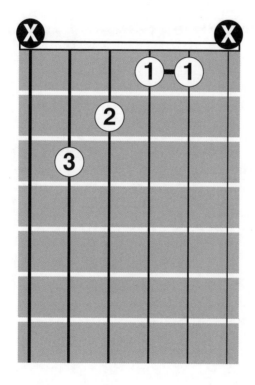

Augmented chords are neither major nor minor. They have an 'open', anticipatory quality and are frequently used to create expectation – which can be resolved by a following major chord. C+ is particularly hard to play cleanly so try D+ (see page 96) before dismissing this unusual chord.

C°

C Diminished

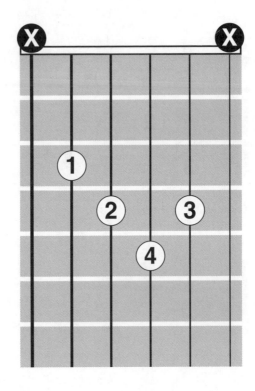

Diminished chords have a distinctive characteristic best described as suspenseful, but they are difficult to finger and of limited use. They are rarely found in pop or rock music but used in isolation – such as at the beginning or end of a song or at a transitional point – they can be very effective. As with augmented chords, the beginner would do well to learn two or three of the simpler shapes to spice up their musical vocabulary.

Csus2

C Suspended 2nd

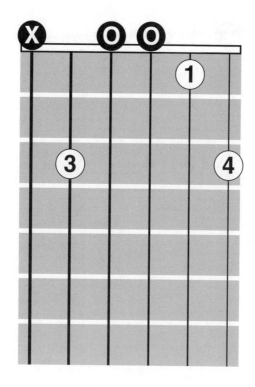

Suspended chords are so called because the third note has been suspended or substituted by the second note above the root. This gives the chord a smooth, dreamy quality which has been used to great effect by The Beatles and Oasis in particular, but also by The Edge of U2 who used it with guitar echo effects to create space and an unconventional tone outside the usual major/minor keys of rock music.

C

C#/Db

D

D#/Eb

E

F

F#/Gb

G

G#/Ab

A

A#/Bb

B

Csus4

C Suspended 4th

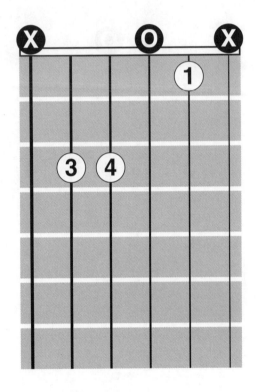

In a suspended 4th, the second note of the chord has been replaced by a note a fourth above the root. As with suspended 2nd chords, the suspended 4th is often used for a particular effect to heighten a sense of otherworldliness. Beginners can ignore both, but learning the easier shapes could come in useful for songwriting, or if you are intending to play more sophisticated music outside of mainstream rock, pop and blues.

C5

C Power Chord

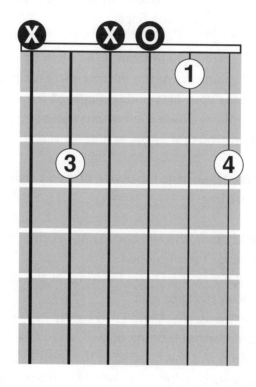

These stripped down, simplified chords are technically neutral, being neither major nor minor, and as such are essential for rock guitarists who would find full chords too muddy and indistinct when played on electric guitar, particularly at high volume. By removing the third note in each chord an interval known as a perfect 5th is created, giving a clear, spacious and powerful tone that can be thickened by distortion. (For more on power chords see overleaf.)

One-finger power chords

To play heavy power chords in a simplified version tune the low E string down to D (using a tuner or the open D string which is an octave higher as a reference). Now you can play power chords with just one finger.

- Play D5 by striking the bottom three open strings only.
- Play E5 by holding down the bottom three strings at the third fret using your first (index) finger as if it was a barre.
- Play F5 by holding down the bottom three strings at the fifth fret using the first finger as a barre and so on.

Alternative one-finger power chords using standard tuning

- For G5 hold down the top two strings at the third fret and play the G and D strings open.
- For A5 hold down the D and G strings at the second fret and play the A string open.
- For E5 hold down the A and D strings at the second fret and play the bottom E string open.
- For D5 hold down the B string at the third fret, the G string at the second fret and play the bottom D and A strings open.

Note that these are not 'moveable shapes' (these are listed on pages 38–51).

Cmaj6

C Major 6th

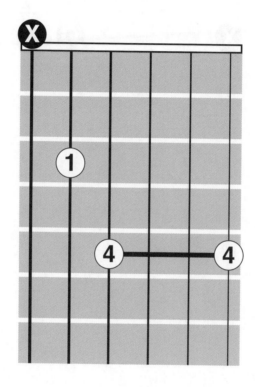

Major 6th chords have an unresolved quality closely associated with The Beatles' early songs and therefore are rarely used in contemporary pop, but if you intend to play songs by other artists (particularly early- to mid-1960s pop) then you will need to learn these. Some major 6th chords have simple alternate fingerings.

Minor 6ths are so rarely featured in popular music that they can be omitted.

Cmaj7
C Major 7th

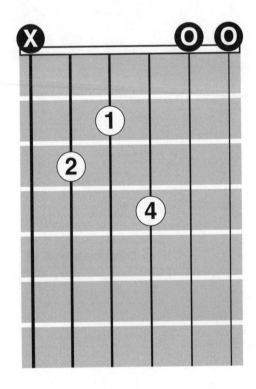

Major 7th chords are created by adding the seventh note of the scale to create a stepping-stone effect. They can be considered as 'passing' chords, used sparingly as a transition from one chord to another. Example sequence: C major 7th, F major, G major, C major.

Cmaj7

C Major 7th
(alternative version)

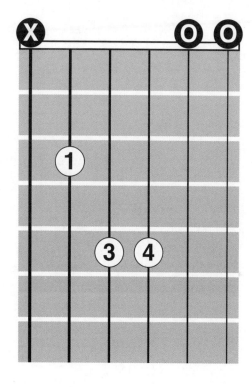

C# / Db

D

D# / Eb

E

F

F# / Gb

G

G# / Ab

A

A# / Bb

B

C7

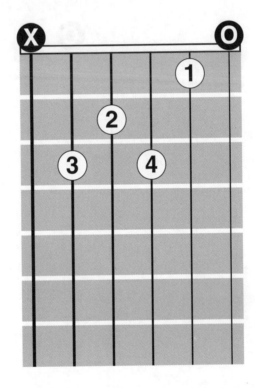

These passing or transitional chords add a seventh note a tone below the root and so are similar in character to major 7th chords – although they have a noticeably different voicing or weight on the lower notes of the chord.

Cm7

C Minor 7th

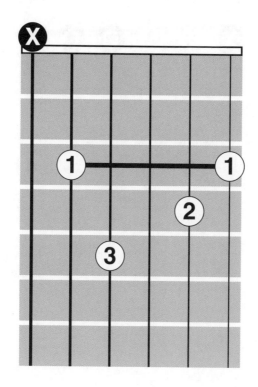

Adding a seventh note a tone below the root makes a minor chord sound more pensive than sad. Substituting a minor 7th chord for a straight minor chord can enhance the reflective or wistful nature of the lyrics and can add a touch of sophistication to a conventional major-minor chord sequence.

Cm/maj7

C Minor/Major 7th

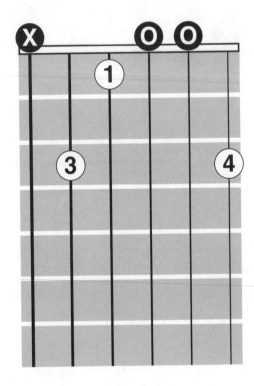

The slightly doomy nature of this chord is best played in isolation, strummed in a space where its full effect can be appreciated. A minor chord with an added seventh note below the root, it is used sparingly to generate atmosphere.

Hear it under the key word 'laughable' in the standard 'My Funny Valentine'.

C°7

C Diminished 7th

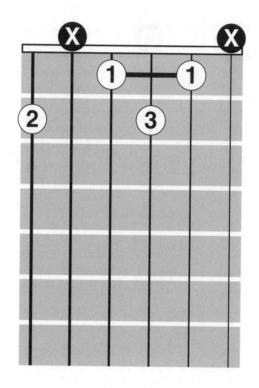

Diminished 7th chords are rare but worth learning as they have a very distinctive 'Spanish' characteristic when played on the guitar. They are created by adding a second minor 3rd to a diminished chord and as such evoke a strange, bitter-sweet flavour to any song in which they feature.

C9

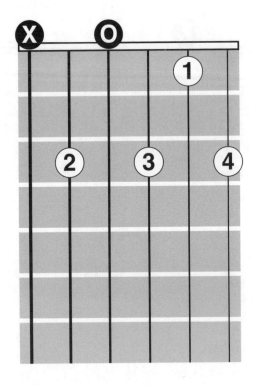

Few rock or pop guitarists will have use for 9th chords, but acoustic players and jazz musicians who want to add subtle shadings to familiar tunes or write their own may find the smoky, late-night club flavour of 9th chords to their taste.

Cmaj9

C Major 9th

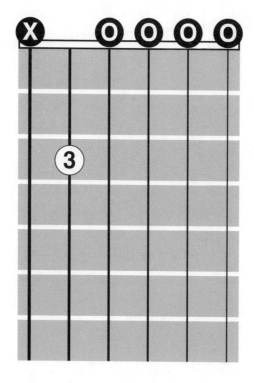

If 'conventional' 9th chords evoke late-night jazz sessions, then major 9ths, with their light, frothy, carefree tone, could be said to conjure up sunny continental café society. This makes them an ideal substitute for a major 7th. The C major 9th is atypical, being simple in the extreme, but other major 9th chords can be very awkward to play. If so, it is permissible to omit the fifth note of the chord and the effect will not be diminished (no pun intended).

Cmaj9

C Major 9th
(alternative version)

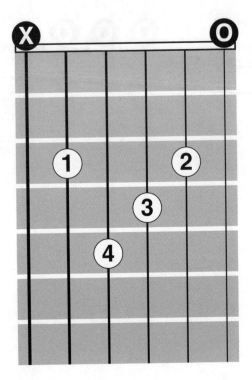

Cmaj9

C Major 9th
(alternative version)

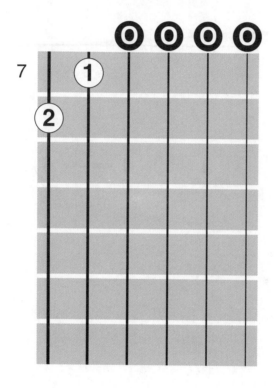

7

Cm9

C Minor 9th

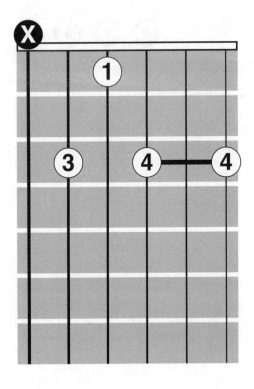

The difference between the colouring of this chord and its less sophisticated alternatives is so subtle that only a trained musician is likely to tell them apart. Minor 9ths are not necessary for the average guitarist to grapple with, which is just as well as they are tortuously difficult to finger. Try Dm9/A and Em9 to see if you can form this type of chord.

Cadd9

C Major Add 9th

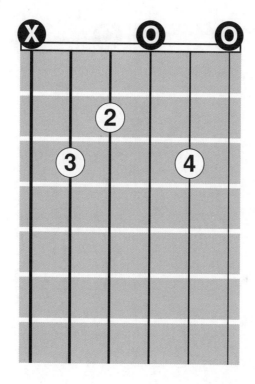

Major add 9ths tend to sound sunny and even bland due to the addition of the ninth note above the octave, strengthening their solidity or conventionality. They are frequently used by American AOR bands such as Foreigner and Boston in their 'radio-friendly' formulaic hits, although singer-songwriters from David Bowie to David Gray have also used them at key moments in their songs to considerable effect.

Cadd9

C Major Add 9th

(alternative version)

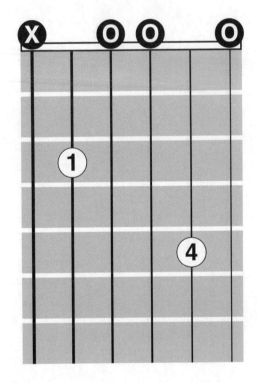

Hear a subtle use of this chord in Morrissey's 'I Have Forgiven Jesus' at the end of the line 'Nothing I can do with this desire'.

Cm add9
C Minor Add 9th

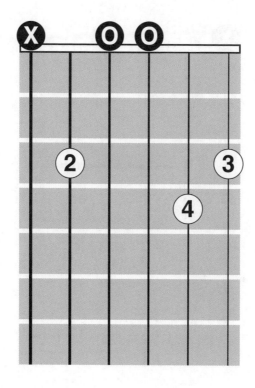

Heavy metal bands such as Black Sabbath, who one might have assumed were musical Neanderthals, were not averse to sneaking in dissonant 'jazz' chords such as these to give their songs a disorientating, nightmarish opening before launching into their trademark skull-crunching power chords. Pink Floyd have also used them to enhance the timeless, ethereal nature of their more psychedelic tracks as they have a delicate, unearthly quality.

Cmaj7

C Major 7th
(moveable shape)

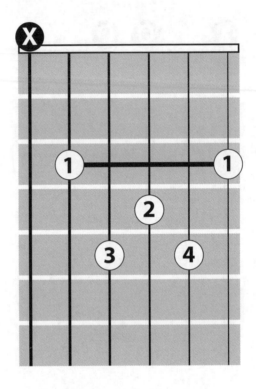

This is a crucial chord shape to learn because, by using the first finger as a barre, you can then slide the shape up and down the fretboard to create any other major 7th chord (C#maj7, Dmaj7, Ebmaj7, Emaj7, Fmaj7, Gbmaj7, Gmaj7, Abmaj7, Amaj7, Bbmaj7 and Bmaj7). NB. The bottom E string is not to be played.

C°

C Diminished
(moveable shape)

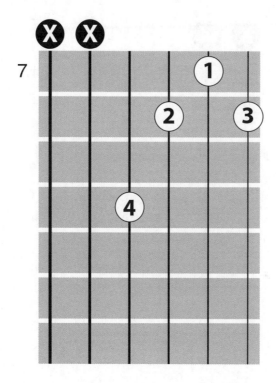

This, too, is an important chord shape to master. Just like Cmaj7, by using the first finger as a barre, you can slide the shape up and down the fretboard to produce any other diminished chord. NB. The bottom strings E and A are not to be played.

Hear the distinctive characteristic of this unusual chord in the Beach Boys' 'God Only Knows' in the first verse accompanying the line 'You never need to doubt it'.

C+

C Augmented
(moveable shape)

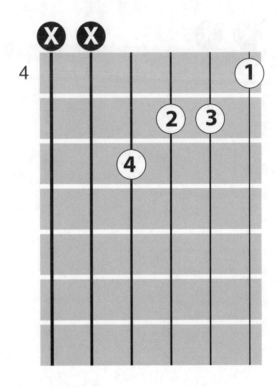

Use the first finger as a barre, then slide up or down the fretboard to produce the other augmented chords. The bottom two strings are not to be played.

Cmaj6

C Major 6th
(moveable shape)

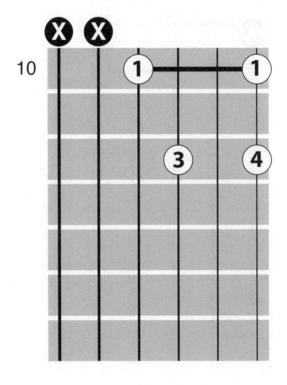

10

Use the first finger as a barre, then slide up or down the fretboard to produce the other major 6th chords. The bottom two strings are not to be played.

Cm6

C Minor 6th
(moveable shape)

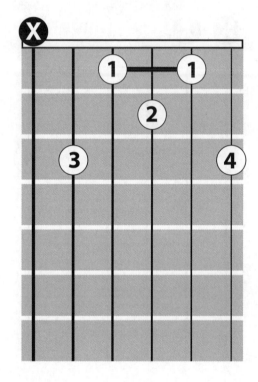

Use the first finger as a barre, then slide up or down the fretboard to produce the other minor 6th chords. The bottom E string is not to be played.

Csus4

C Suspended 4th
(moveable shape)

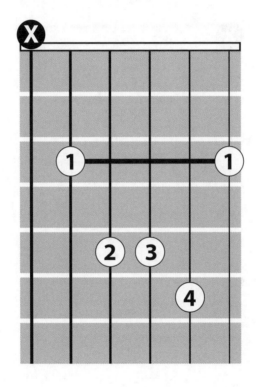

Use the first finger as a barre, then slide up or down the fretboard to produce the other suspended 4th chords. The bottom E string is not to be played.

Csus2

C Suspended 2nd
(moveable shape)

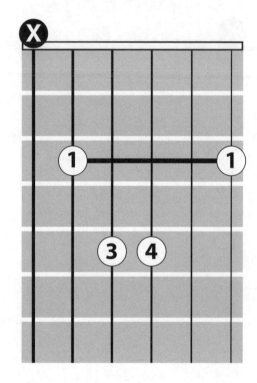

Use the first finger as a barre, then slide up or down the fretboard to produce the other suspended 2nd chords. The bottom E string is not to be played.

C°7

C Diminished 7th
(moveable shape)

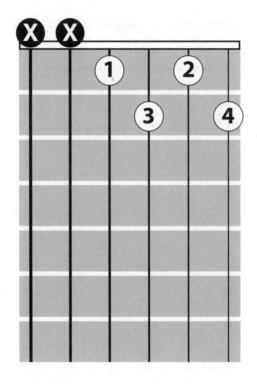

Use the first finger as a barre, then slide up or down the fretboard to produce the other diminished 7th chords. The bottom E and A strings are not to be played.

C7

(moveable shape)

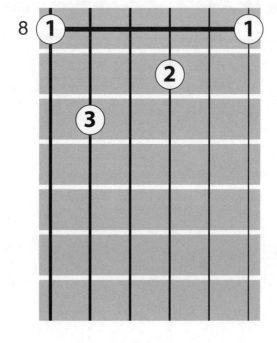

8

Use the first finger as a barre, then slide up or down the fretboard to produce the other 7th chords.

Cm7

C Minor 7th

(moveable shape)

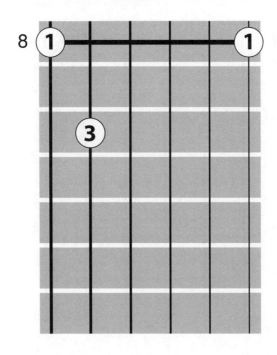

Use the first finger as a barre, then slide up or down the fretboard to produce the other minor 7th chords.

C♯/D♭

D

D♯/E♭

E

F

F♯/G♭

G

G♯/A♭

A

A♯/B♭

B

Cm/maj7

C Minor/Major 7th

(moveable shape)

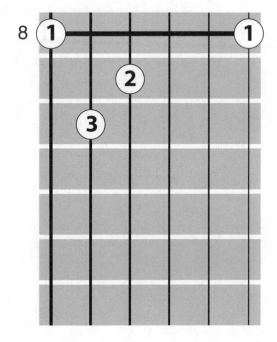

Use the first finger as a barre, then slide up or down the fretboard to produce the other minor/major 7th chords.

Cadd9

C Add 9th
(moveable shape)

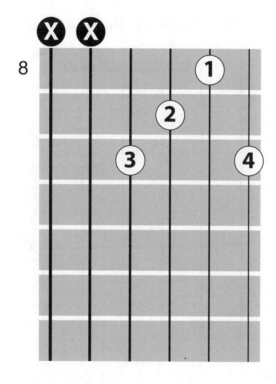

Use the first finger as a barre, then slide up or down the fretboard to produce the other add 9th chords. The bottom E and A strings are not to be played.

Cmaj9

C Major 9th
(moveable shape)

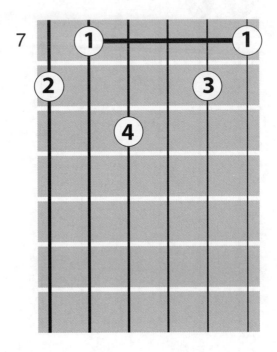

Use the first finger as a barre, then slide up or down the fretboard to produce the other major 9th chords.

C9

(moveable shape)

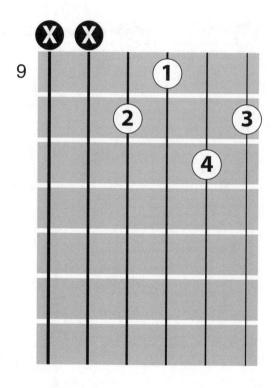

9

Use the first finger as a barre, then slide up or down the
fretboard to produce the other 9th chords. The bottom E and
A strings are not to be played.

Cmaj11

C Major 11th

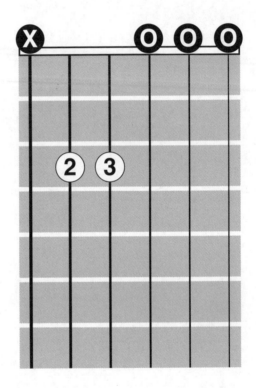

Cmaj11

C Major 11th
(alternative version)

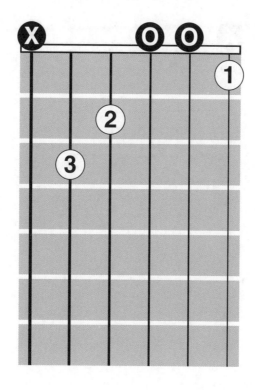

Cmaj11

C Major 11th

(alternative version)

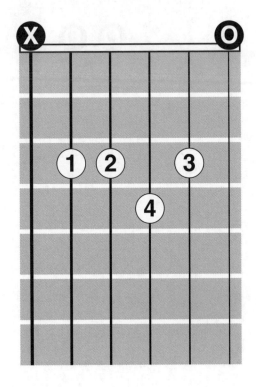

Cmaj11

C Major 11th
(alternative version)

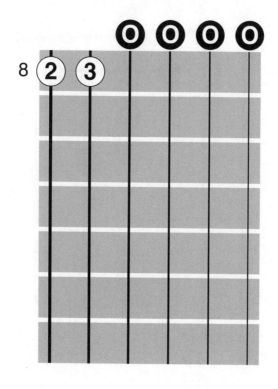

Cm11
C Minor 11th

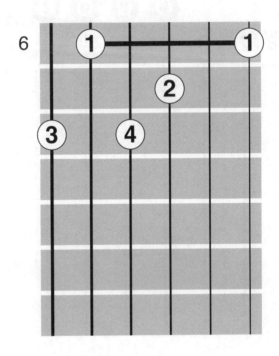

C#maj/D♭maj

C# or D♭ Major

(basic version)

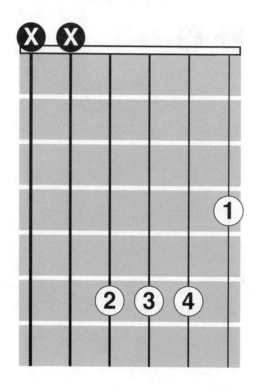

C♯maj/D♭maj

C♯ or D♭ Major

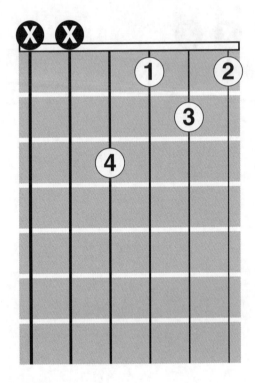

This chord can be simplified by omitting the fourth finger from the D string to create a major triad.

C#maj/D♭maj

C# or D♭ Major
(first inversion)

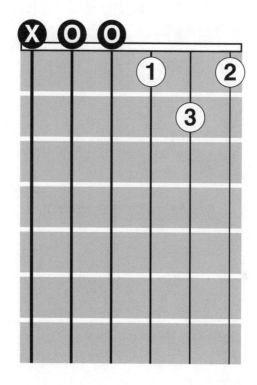

This is the D major triad moved down one fret. It is ideal for arpeggio playing but without the fourth string it lacks weight. You can thicken it by playing the third fret on the D string with your fourth finger, if you can make the stretch.

C♯maj/D♭maj

C♯ or D♭ Major

(barre chord)

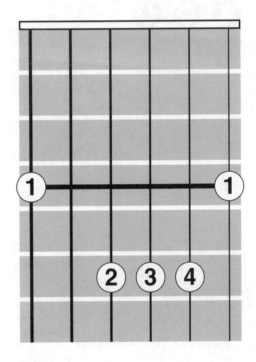

C#m/Dbm

C# or Db Minor
(simplified version)

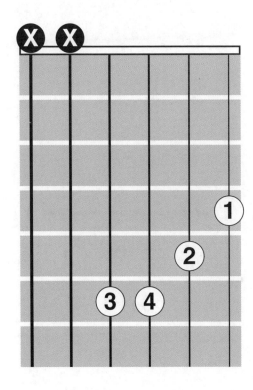

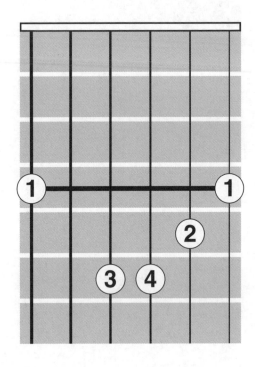

C#m/D♭m

C# or D♭ Minor
(barre chord)

C#+/Db+

C# or Db Augmented

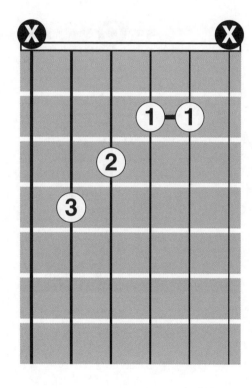

C
C#/Db
D
D#/Eb
E
F
F#/Gb
G
G#/Ab
A
A#/Bb
B

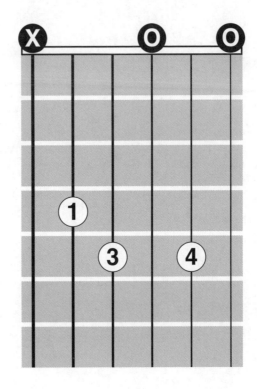

C#°/Db°

C# or Db Diminished

C#sus2/D♭sus2

C# or D♭ Suspended 2nd

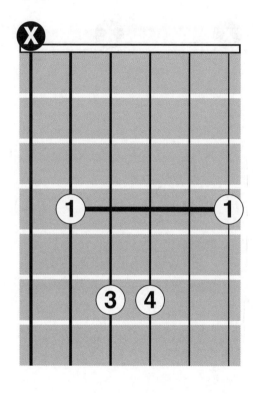

C#sus4/Dbsus4

C# or Db Suspended 4th

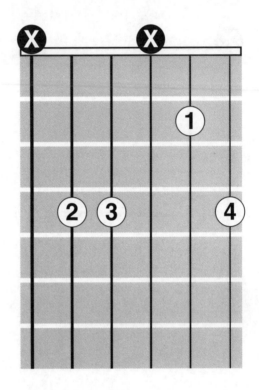

C#5/D♭5

C# or D♭ Power Chord

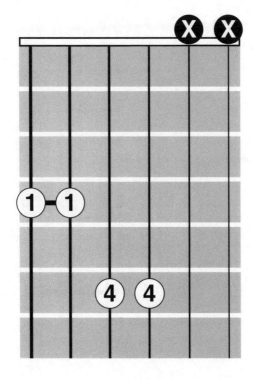

C#maj6/D♭maj6

C# or D♭ Major 6th

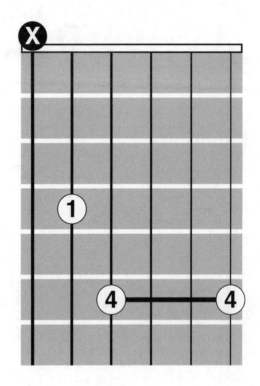

C#maj7/D♭maj7

C# or D♭ Major 7th

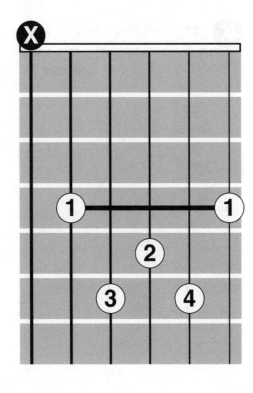

C♯maj7/D♭maj7

C♯ or D♭ Major 7th

(alternative version)

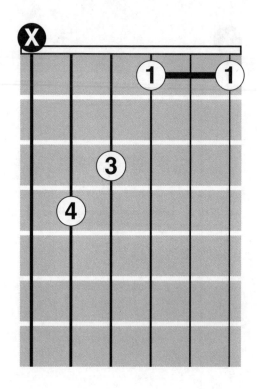

C#7/Db7

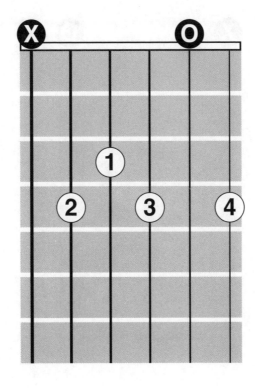

C#m7/Dbm7

C# or Db Minor 7th

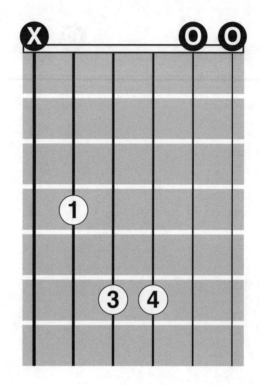

C#m/maj7/D♭m/maj7
C# or D♭ Minor/Major 7th

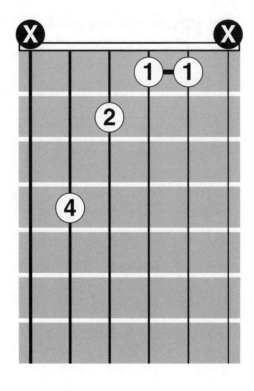

C#°7/Db°7

C# or Db Diminished 7th

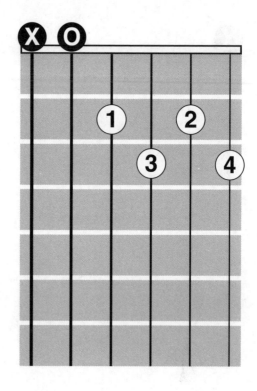

C♯°7/D♭°7

C♯ or D♭ Diminished 7th
(alternative version)

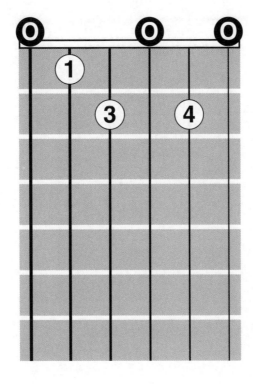

C#9/D♭9

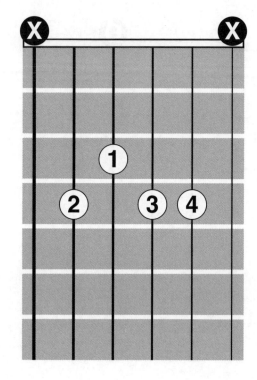

C#9/D♭9

(alternative version)

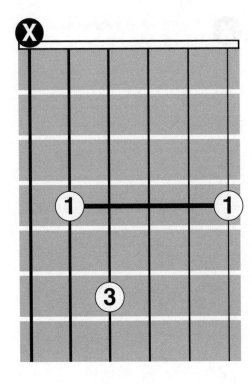

C#maj9/D♭maj9

C# or D♭ Major 9th

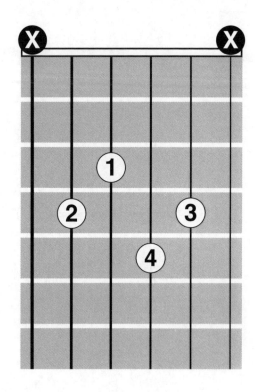

C#m9/D♭m9

C# or D♭ Minor 9th

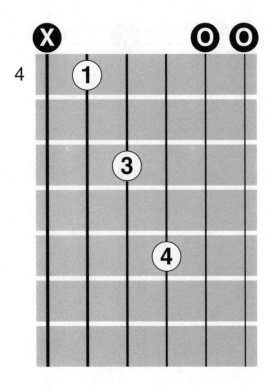

C#add9/D♭add9

C# or D♭ Add 9th

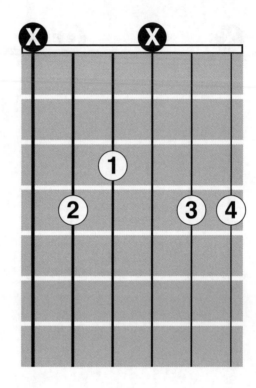

C#m add9/D♭m add9

C# or D♭ Minor Add 9th

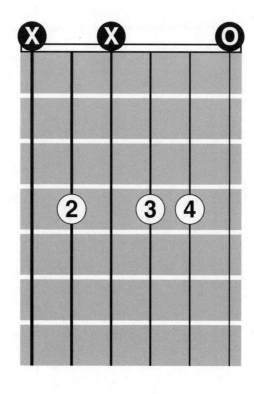

C#maj7add11/Dbmaj7add11

C# or Db Major 7th Add 11

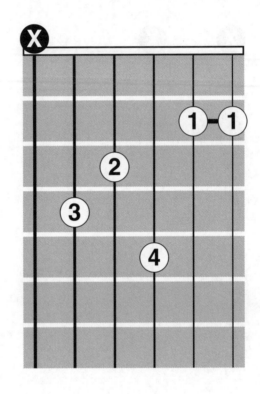

C#maj7add11/D♭maj7add11

C# or D♭ Major 7th Add 11

(alternative version)

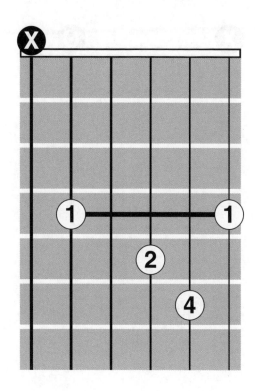

C#m7add11/Dbm7add11

C# or Db Minor 7th Add 11

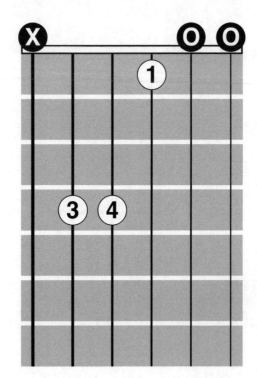

C#m11/D♭m11
C# or D♭ Minor 11th

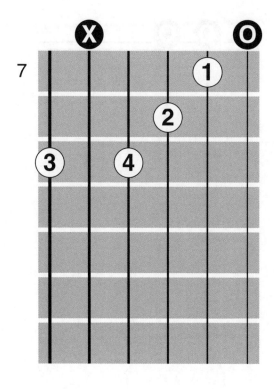

Dmaj

D Major Triad
(simplified version)

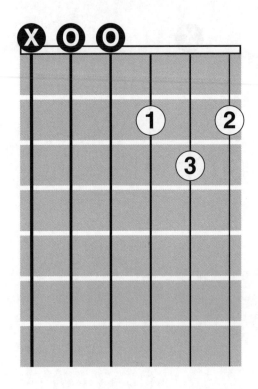

Strictly speaking, this is the second inversion of Dmaj (denoted as D/A in many songbooks) but it is the easiest version to learn. Hear how effective a few chords can be in David Bowie's 'All The Young Dudes' where Dmaj begins each verse, then mutates into Dmaj7 before changing to Bm and Bm7.

Dmaj

D Major Triad
(alternative version)

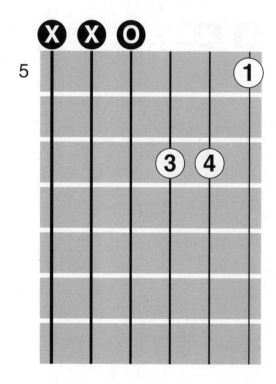

This is only slightly more difficult to finger for the beginner than the chord opposite but it can be a useful alternative voicing. It will provide a lighter tone when accompanying another guitar playing the simplified version lower down the neck. If you see the notation D/A in a songbook it simply means that you can play the bottom A string open or the D major triad on the previous page.

Dmaj

D Major
(first inversion)

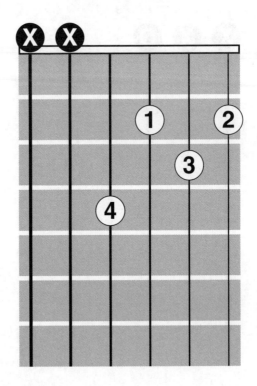

This fuller version of Dmaj adds a second F♯ on the D string and will be indicated in many songbooks as D/F♯. Hear what the Beatles made of the simple D, C, G three-chord trick in 'Norwegian Wood' where these chords form the verse.

D/A

D Major/A
(second inversion)

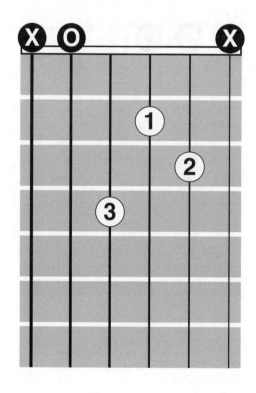

C

C#/Db

D

D#/Eb

E

F

F#/Gb

G

G#/Ab

A

A#/Bb

B

D/A

D Major/A
(alternative second inversion)

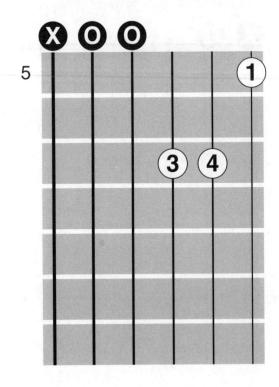

Dmaj

D Major

(barre chord)

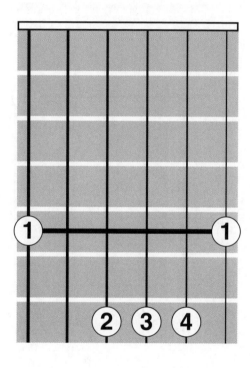

Dmaj

D Major
(barre chord alternative version)

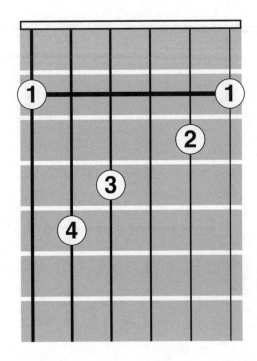

Dm

D Minor
(simplified version)

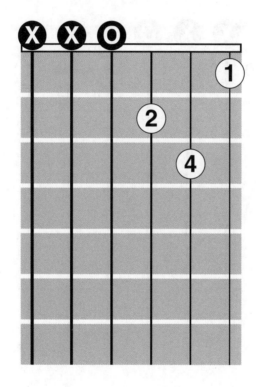

Hear this chord in the first line of each verse of Bon Jovi's 'Blaze of Glory'. The only other chords you will need to play this song are C, G and Fmaj.

Dm

D Minor
(alternative version)

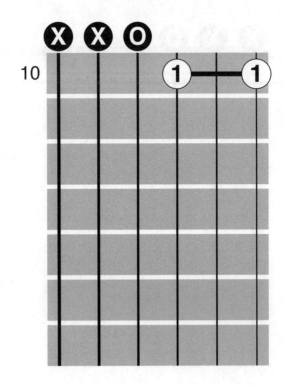

Dm

D Minor
(barre chord)

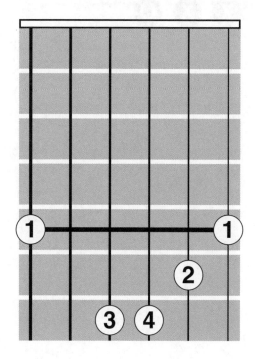

Even Neo-Prog masters Muse who indulge in complex chord
patterns occasionally restrict themselves to conventional
chords – as in 'Sing For Absolution', which evolves from Dm
to A♯, E and A major in the verses, and features only Cmaj and
Gm in the uplifting chorus.

C

C♯/D♭

D

D♯/E♭

E

F

F♯/G♭

G

G♯/A♭

A

A♯/B♭

B

D+

D Augmented

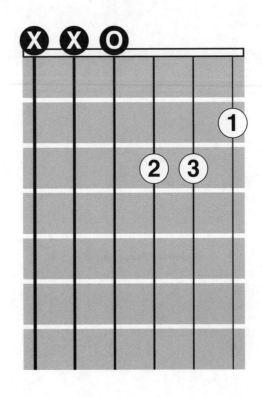

D°

D Diminished

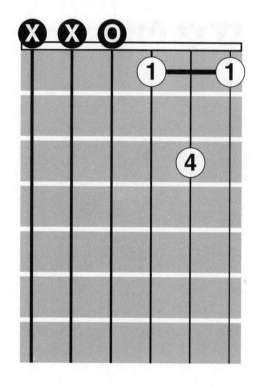

Dsus2

D Suspended 2nd

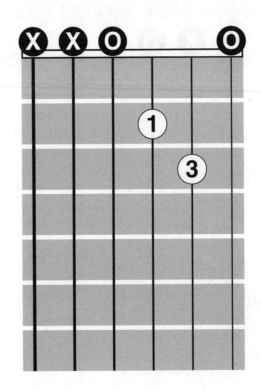

Dsus4

D Suspended 4th

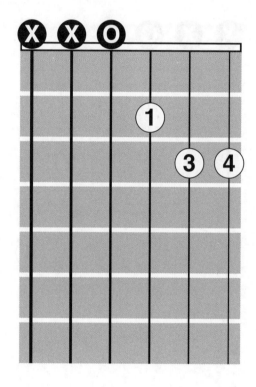

Hear this chord add a touch of Broadway to the end of each verse of 'Raindrops Keep Falling On My Head' by Burt Bacharach.

D5

D Power Chord

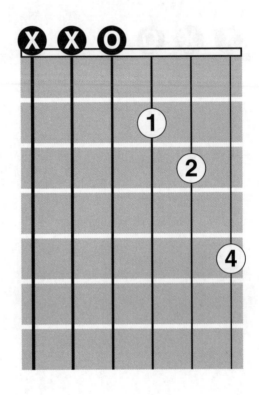

Dmaj6

D Major 6th

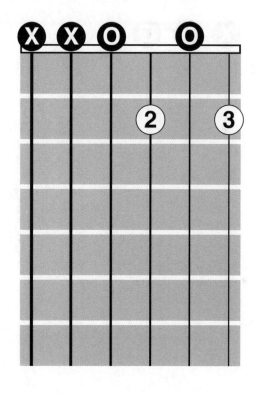

Dmaj6

D Major 6th
(alternative version)

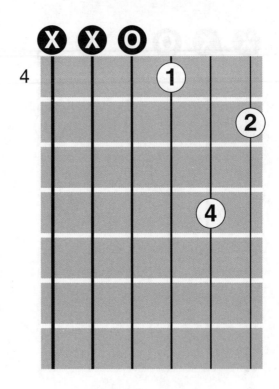

Dmaj7

D Major 7th

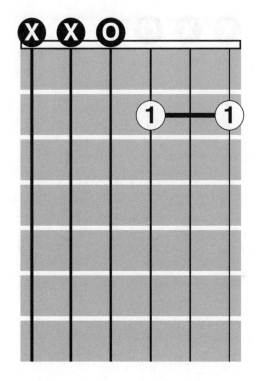

Hear how this chord can generate suspense and tension when used at the end of the line 'get on my knees and pray' in 'Won't Get Fooled Again' by The Who.

Dmaj7

D Major 7th
(alternative version)

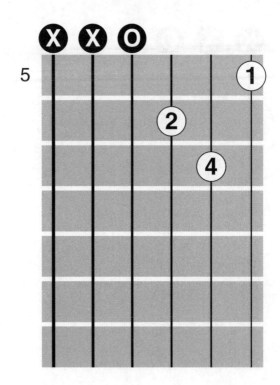

D7

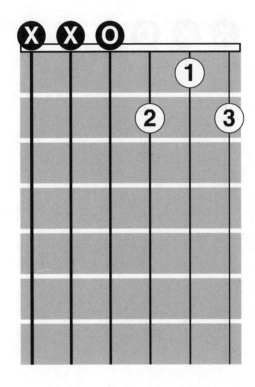

Listen to 'In The Presence Of The Lord' by Blind Faith and hear how D7 and G7 add a bluesy tone under the words 'but I can open any door'.

D7

(alternative version)

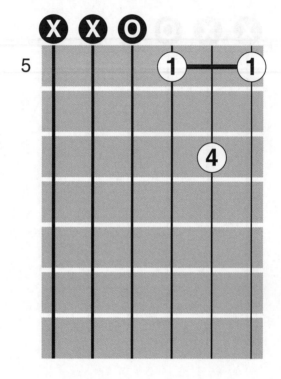

Dm7

D Minor 7th

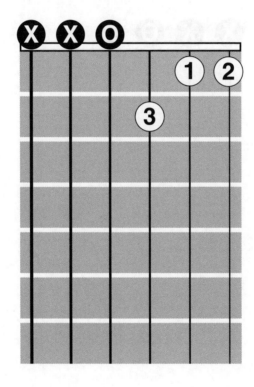

Dm7

D Minor 7th
(alternative version)

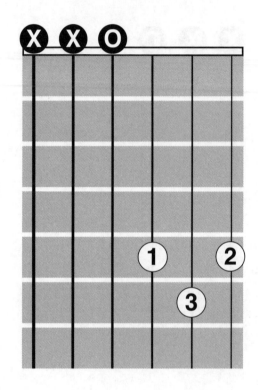

Dm/maj7

D Minor/Major 7th

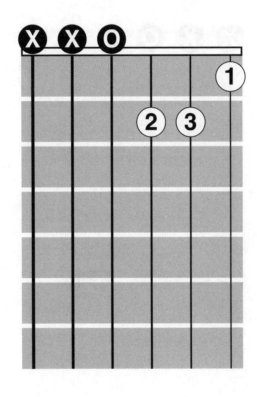

D°7

D Diminished 7th

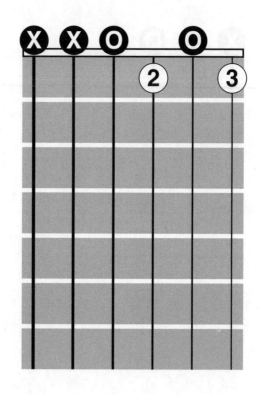

D9

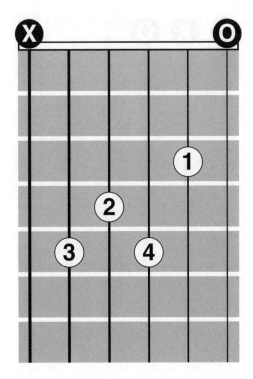

C

C♯/D♭

D

D♯/E♭

E

F

F♯/G♭

G

G♯/A♭

A

A♯/B♭

B

Chuck Berry used a D9 at the end of the chorus of 'Roll Over Beethoven' to add a subtle blues inflection to a basic 12-bar blues in D. The other two chords in the song are G and A major.

D9

(alternative version)

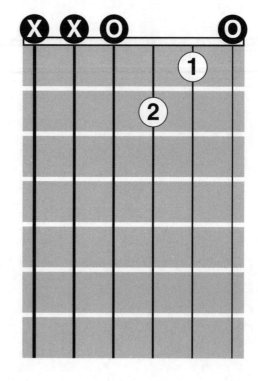

Dmaj9

D Major 9th
(simplified version with no 3rd)

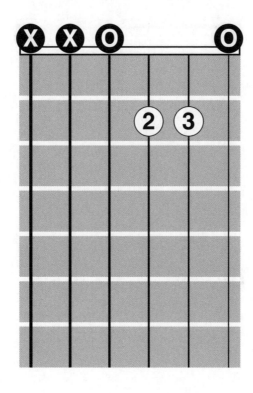

Dmaj9

D Major 9th

(full version)

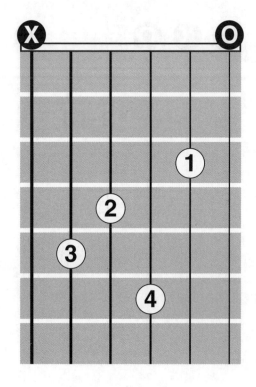

Dmaj9

D Major 9th
(alternative version)

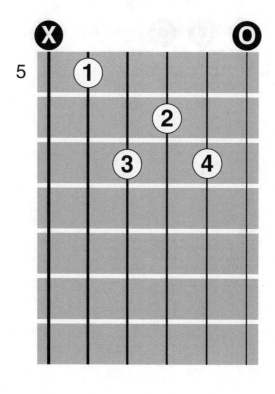

5

C

C#/Db

D

D#/Eb

E

F

F#/Gb

G

G#/Ab

A

A#/Bb

B

Dmaj9/A

D Major 9th /A

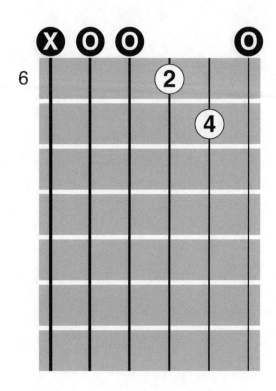

Dm9/A

D Minor 9th/A

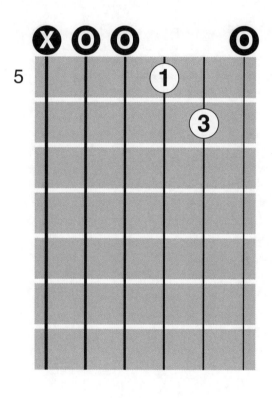

5

C

C#/Db

D

D#/Eb

E

F

F#/Gb

G

G#/Ab

A

A#/Bb

B

Dm9

D Minor 9th

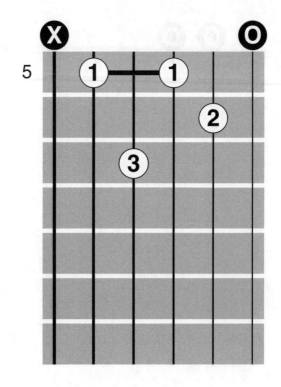

Dadd9

D Add 9th

(simplified version)

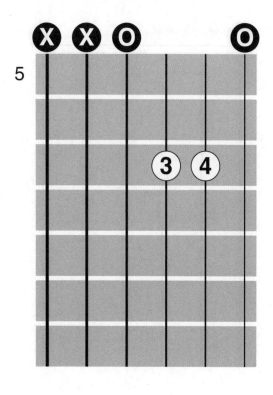

Dadd9

D Add 9th

(alternative version)

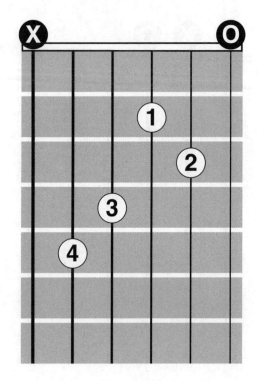

Dm add9

D Minor Add 9th

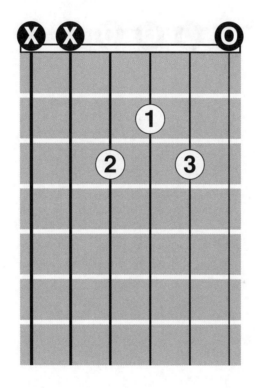

Strictly speaking this is the first inversion, Dm add9/F, but as it is the only practical (easily playable) version of the chord, it is offered as the only version.

Dmaj11/F#

D Major 11th/F#
(simplified version)

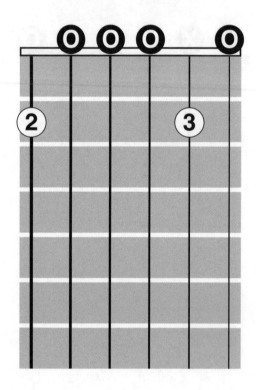

Dmaj11

D Major 11th
(alternative version)

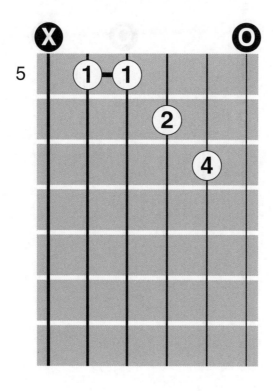

Dmaj11

D Major 11th
(alternative version)

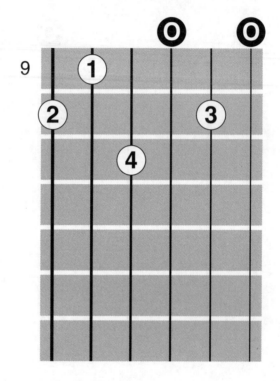

Dm7add11/A

D Minor 7th Add 11/A

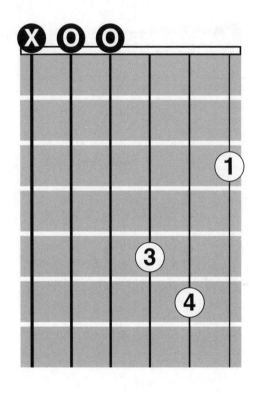

C#/D♭

D

D#/E♭

E

F

F#/G♭

G

G#/A♭

A

A#/B♭

B

Dm7add11

D Minor 7th Add 11

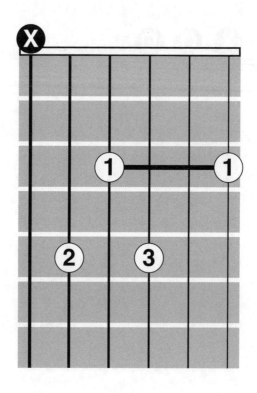

Dm11

D Minor 11th

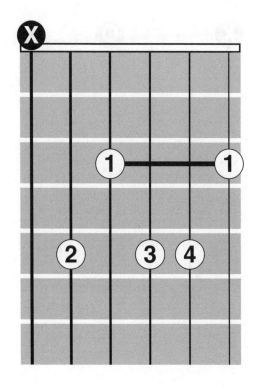

Dm11

D Minor 11th
(alternative version)

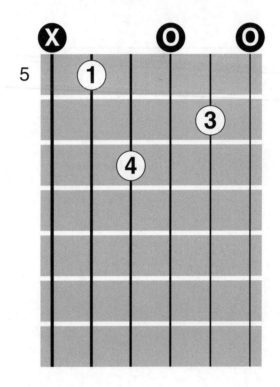

Dm11

D Minor 11th
(alternative version)

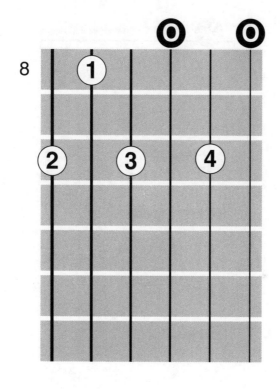

8

C

C#/Db

D

D#/Eb

E

F

F#/Gb

G

G#/Ab

A

A#/Bb

B

D#maj/Ebmaj

D# or Eb Major
(simplified version)

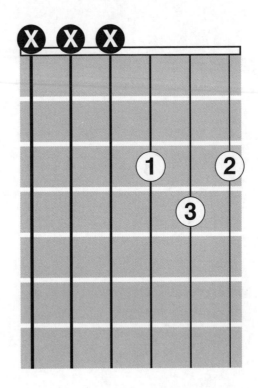

D#maj/E♭maj

D# or E♭ Major
(first inversion)

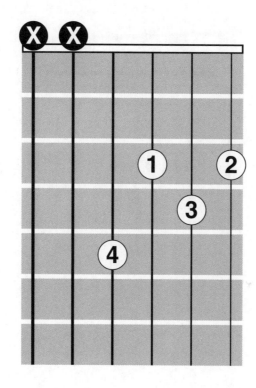

This will be noted as E♭/G in many songbooks.

D#maj/Ebmaj

D# or Eb Major

(barre chord)

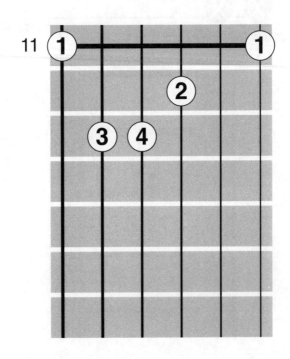

D♯maj/E♭maj

D♯ or E♭ Major
(barre chord alternative version)

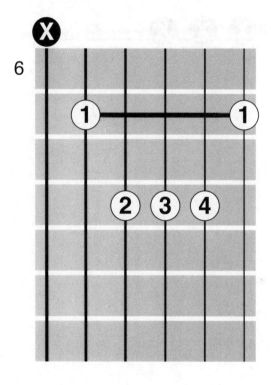

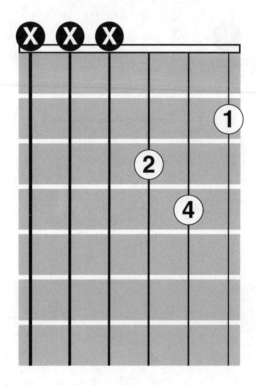

D#m/E♭m

D# or E♭ Minor
(simplified version)

This chord is a temporary solution, useful only for those who have not mastered barre chords, as it has no fourth bass note, and so will sound thin. The sooner you are familiar with the barre chord version on the following page, the better.

D♯m/E♭m

D♯ or E♭ Minor
(barre chord)

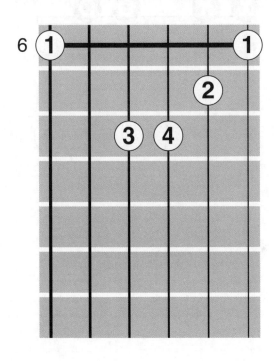

6

C

C#/Db

D

D#/Eb

E

F

F#/Gb

G

G#/Ab

A

A#/Bb

B

D#+/Eb+

D# or Eb Augmented

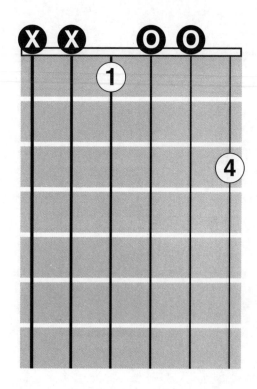

D#°/E♭°

D# or E♭ Diminished

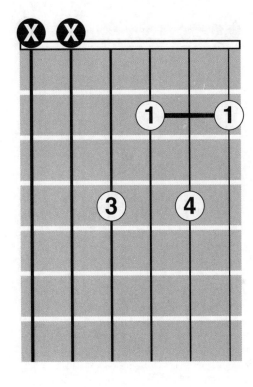

D#sus2/Ebsus2

D# or Eb Suspended 2nd

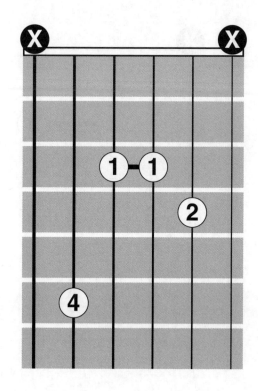

D#sus2/E♭sus2

D# or E♭ Suspended 2nd
(alternative version)

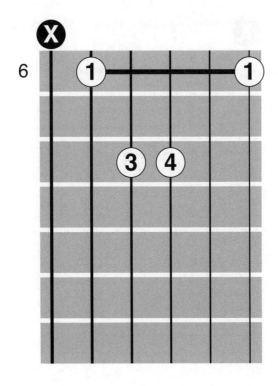

This version is considerably easier to hold down than that on the previous page.

D#sus4/E♭sus4

D# or E♭ Suspended 4th

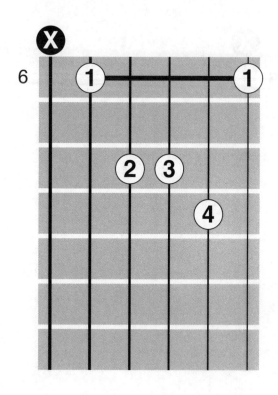

D#5/E♭5

D# or E♭ Power Chord

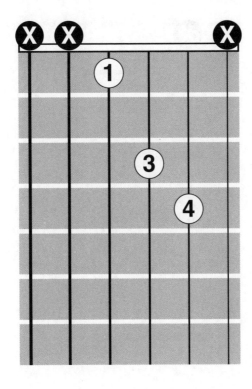

D#maj6/E♭maj6

D# or E♭ Major 6th

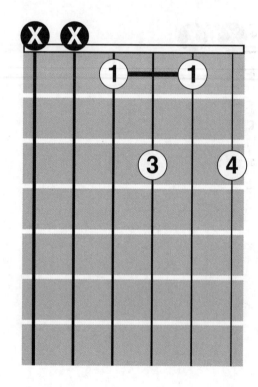

C

C#/D♭

D

D#/E♭

E

F

F#/G♭

G

G#/A♭

A

A#/B♭

B

D♯maj7/E♭maj7

D♯ or E♭ Major 7th

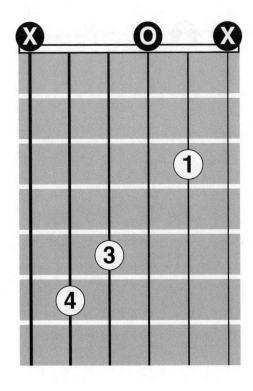

D#7/E♭7

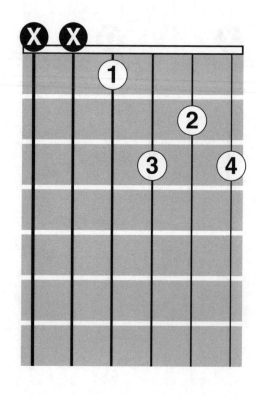

D#m7/E♭m7

D# or E♭ Minor 7th

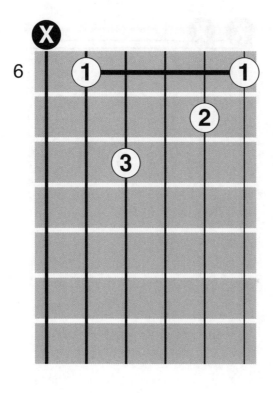

D#m/maj7/Ebm/maj7

D# or Eb Minor/Major 7th

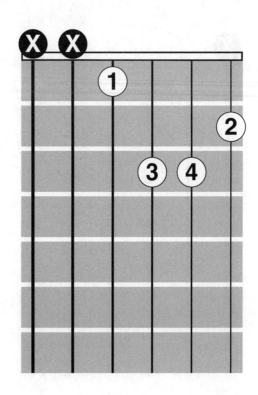

D#°7/E♭°7

D# or E♭ Diminished 7th

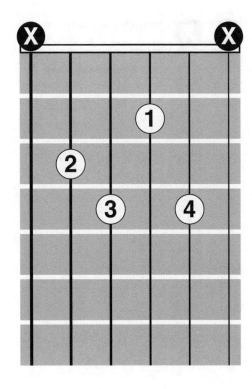

D♯9/E♭9

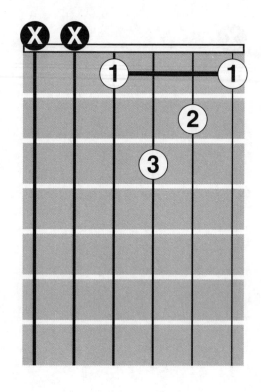

D♯9/E♭9

(alternative version)

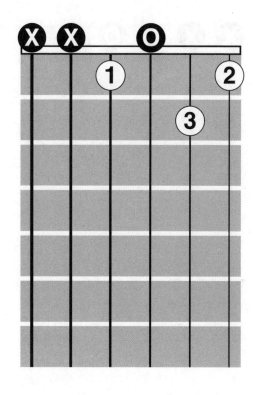

D#maj9/E♭maj9

D# or E♭ Major 9th

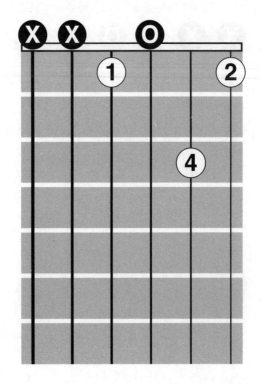

D#m9/E♭m9

D# or E♭ Minor 9th

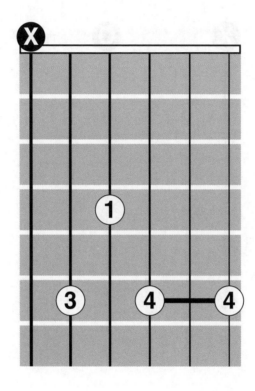

D#add9/Ebadd9

D# or Eb Add 9th

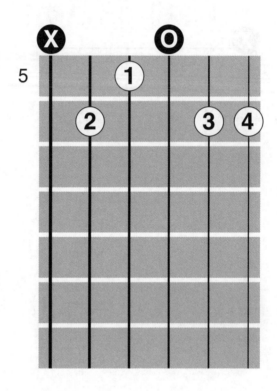

D#m add9/E♭m add9

D# or E♭ Minor Add 9th

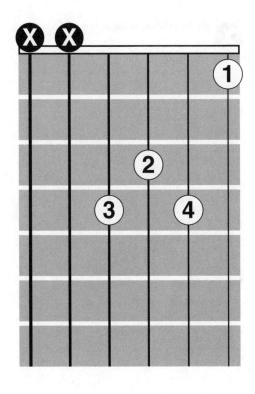

D#maj7add11/Ebmaj7add11

D# or Eb Major 7th Add 11

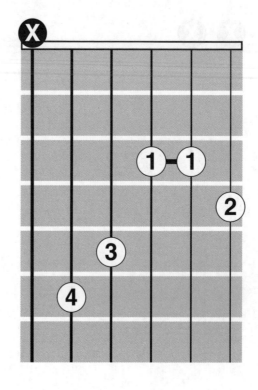

D#maj11/E♭maj11

D# or E♭ Major 11th

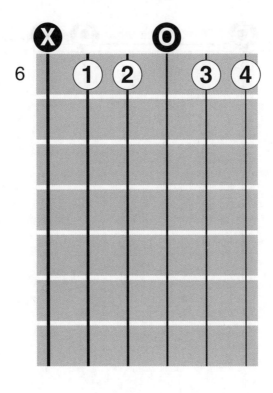

6

Emaj

E Major Triad
(basic version)

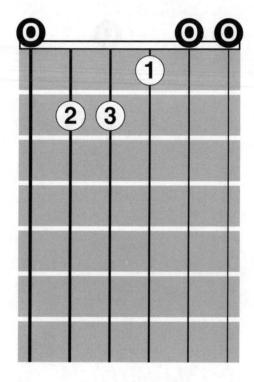

If you learn this chord you are one third of the way towards being able to play most of the early 1950s and 1960s rock classics, most of the entire punk catalogue and any 12-bar blues you care to name. All you need now are A major and B major and you have the basic three-chord trick which is the cornerstone of rock, pop and blues.

Emaj

E Major
(alternative version)

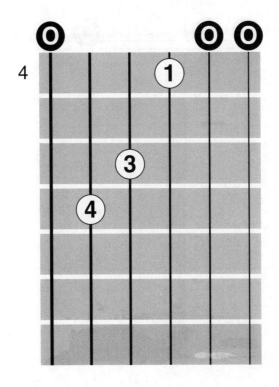

You will need long fingers to make this stretch practical but it can be a useful alternate voicing if you want Emaj higher up the neck.

Emaj

E Major

(first inversion)

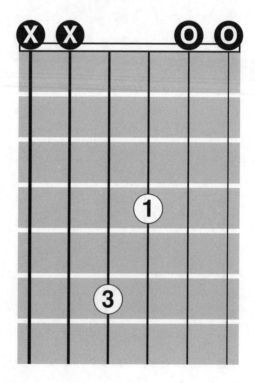

A sparser version, typically denoted as E/G#. Be careful to avoid striking the bottom two strings.

Emaj

E Major
(barre chord)

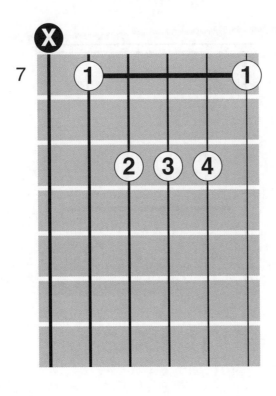

Emaj

E Major
(barre chord alternative version)

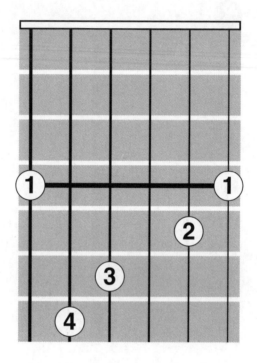

Em

E Minor
(basic version)

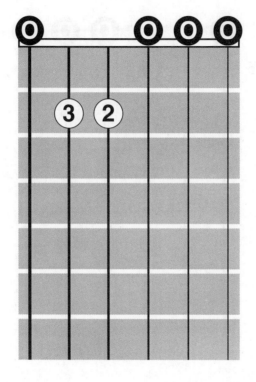

One of the easiest chords in the book and an essential one to pick up from day one. Its relative major is C. Hear how effective this simple progression can be on one of the most covered songs in pop, Leonard Cohen's 'Hallelujah'.

C

C#/Db

D

D#/Eb

E

F

F#/Gb

G

G#/Ab

A

A#/Bb

B

Em

E Minor
(alternative version)

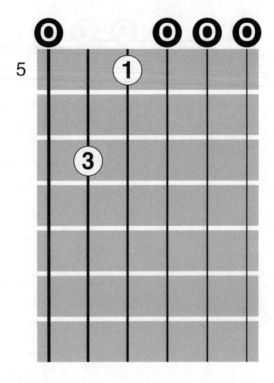

5

A less dense voicing of Em. Play this and then the version on the previous page to appreciate the subtle difference.

Em

E Minor
(barre chord)

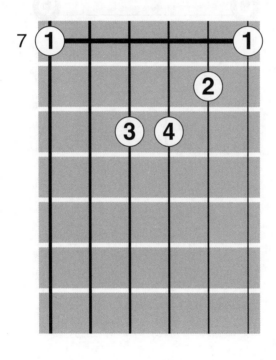

7

C

C♯/D♭

D

D♯/E♭

E

F

F♯/G♭

G

G♯/A♭

A

A♯/B♭

B

E+

E Augmented

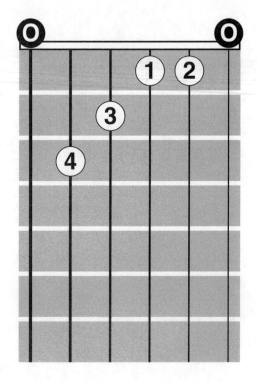

E°

E Diminished

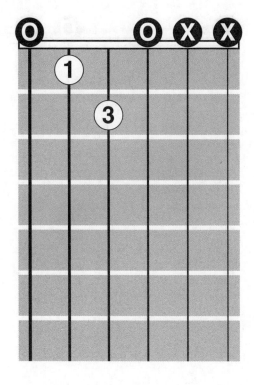

Esus2

E Suspended 2nd

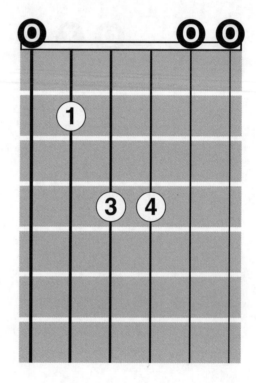

Esus4

E Suspended 4th

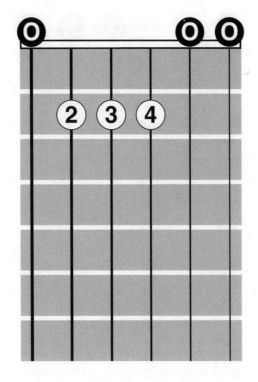

Hear how this chord adds interest to a long, repetitious melody line in Blur's hit 'Parklife' under the words 'habitual voyeur'. The chord before and after it is E major.

E5

E Power Chord

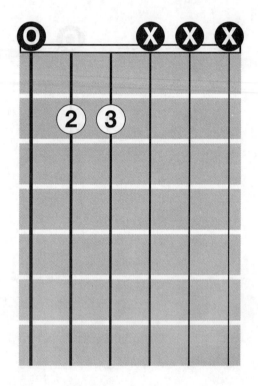

Many heavy metal and heavy rock songs rely exclusively on power chords and riffs which pick notes from the chord. 'Motörhead' by Motörhead is a classic example. The verse is simply E5 to Dmaj and back with G, D and F♯ major for the chorus.

E5

E Power Chord
(alternative version)

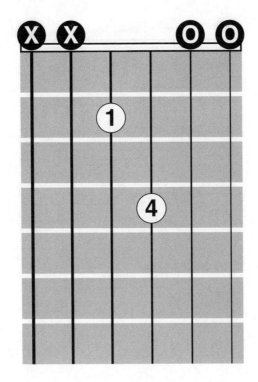

Stripped down to its basic elements, Metallica's 'Enter Sandman' is revealed as being variations on the following power chords: E, A, A#, F, F# and G5.

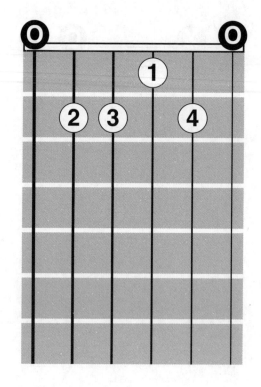

Emaj6

E Major 6th

Emaj6

E Major 6th
(alternative version)

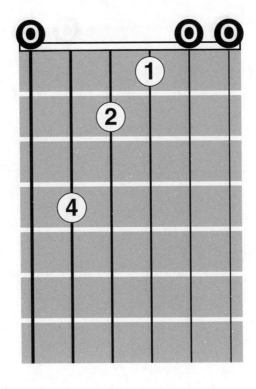

Emaj7

E Major 7th

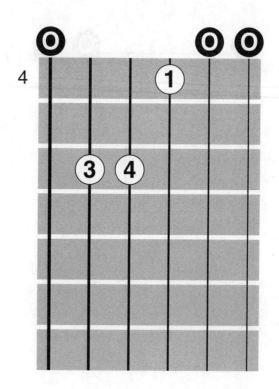

4

172

E7

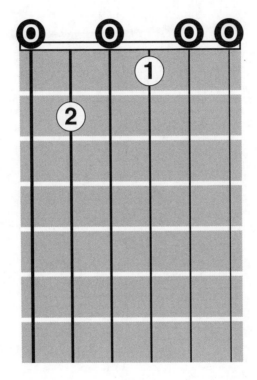

Hear this chord used as a transition from Em to Cmaj in Blur's hit 'Country House' at the end of the phrase 'I'm caught in a rat race'.

E7

(alternative version)

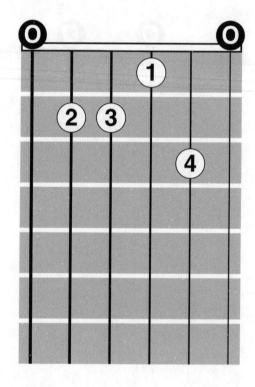

Em7

E Minor 7th

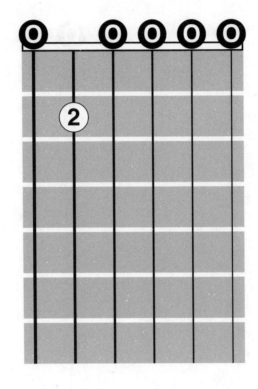

Em/maj7

E Minor/Major 7th

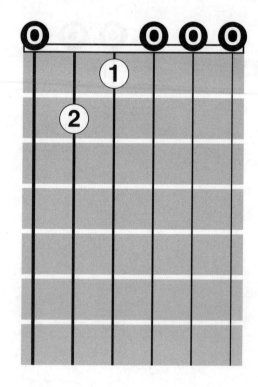

Em/maj7

E Minor/Major 7th
(alternative version)

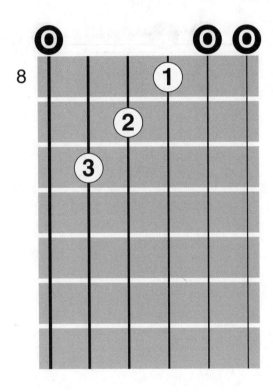

8

E°7

E Diminished 7th

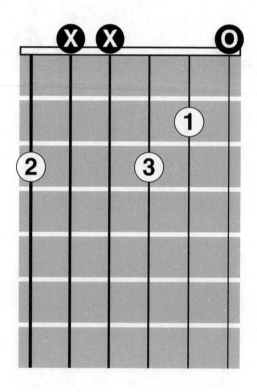

E9

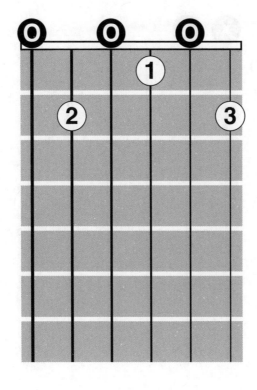

E9

(alternative version)

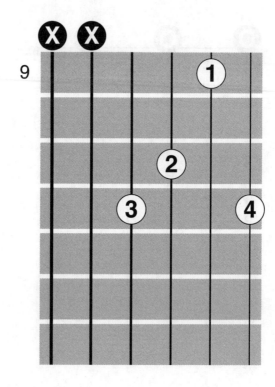

Emaj9

E Major 9th

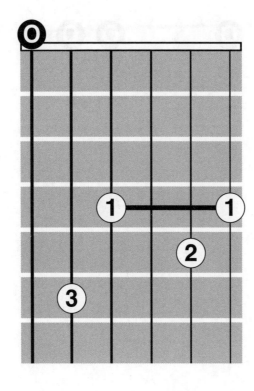

Em9

E Minor 9th

C

C#/Db

D

D#/Eb

E

F

F#/Gb

G

G#/Ab

A

A#/Bb

B

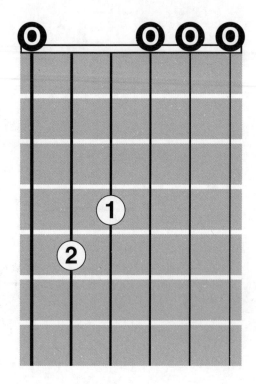

Eadd9

E Add 9th

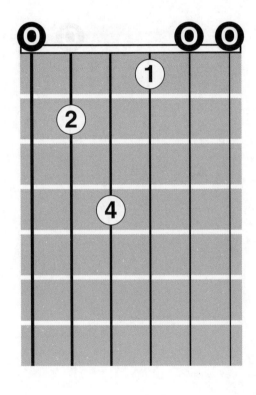

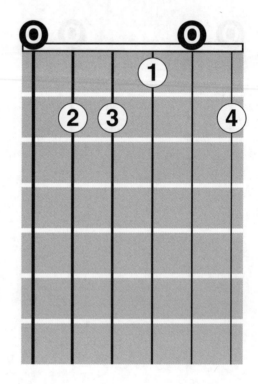

Eadd9

E Add 9th

(alternative version)

Em add9

E Minor Add 9th

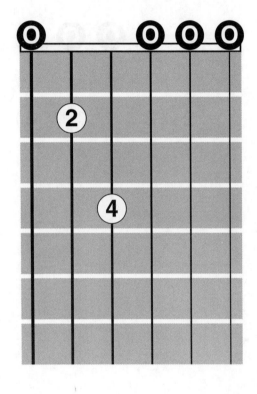

Em add9

E Minor Add 9th

(alternative version)

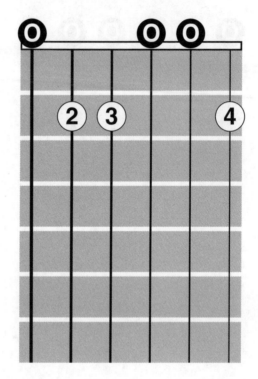

Emaj7add11

E Major 7th Add 11

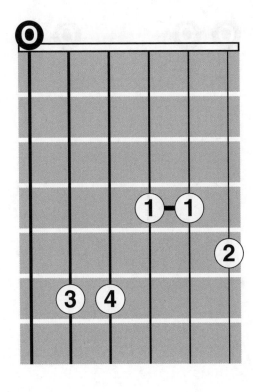

Emaj11

E Major 11th

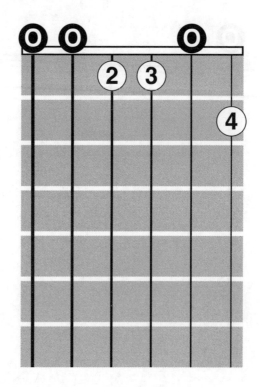

Emaj11

E Major 11th

(alternative version)

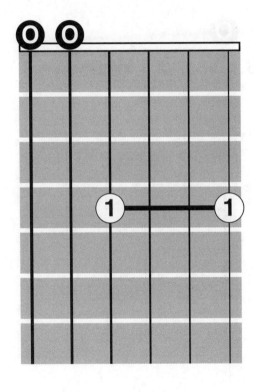

Em7add11

E Minor 7th Add 11

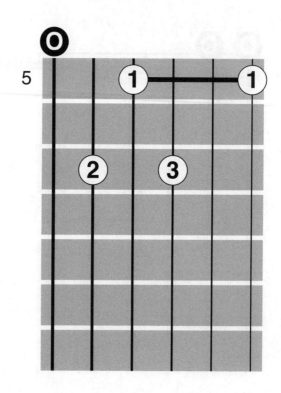

5

Em11

E Minor 11th

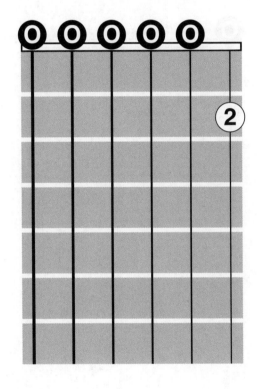

Em11

E Minor 11th

(alternative version)

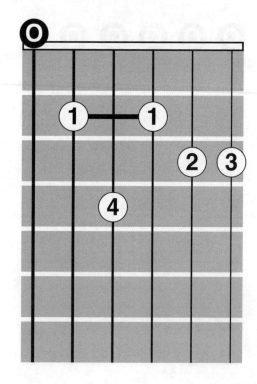

Em11

E Minor 11th
(alternative version)

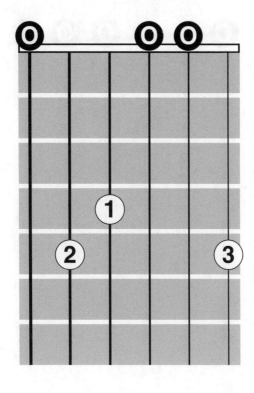

Em11

E Minor 11th

(alternative version)

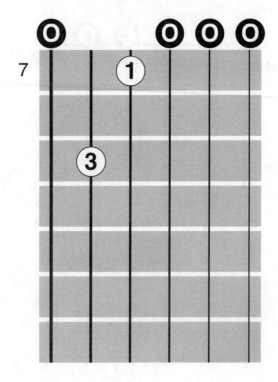

F

F Major
(basic version)

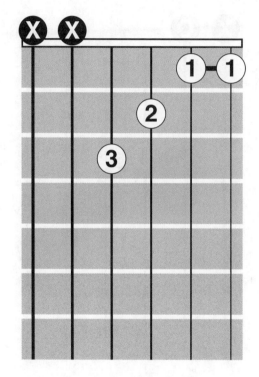

Pressing the first finger down across two frets as indicated on the diagram is not as difficult as it might appear. Include it in your daily practice routine every day for a week and you will be able to make it ring clean and clear.

F/A

F Major/A
(first inversion)

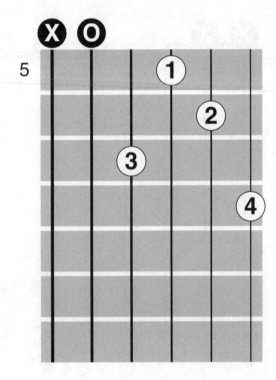

The F major chord on the previous page and its first inversion above are for all practical purposes interchangeable, as are all the simplified versions of the major chords and their fuller first inversions, so at the beginning play whichever version you find more comfortable.

F

F Major
(barre chord)

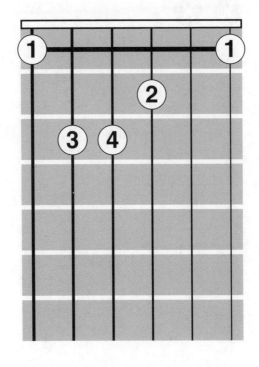

Fm

F Minor
(simplified version)

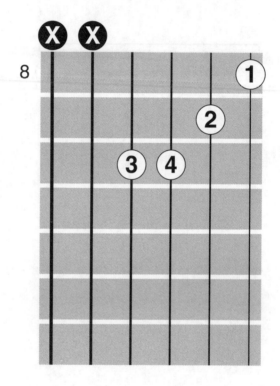

C

C#/Db

D

D#/Eb

E

F

F#/Gb

G

G#/Ab

A

A#/Bb

B

Fm

F Minor
(barre chord)

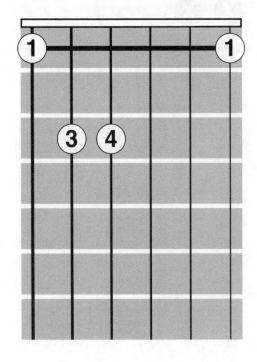

F+

F Augmented

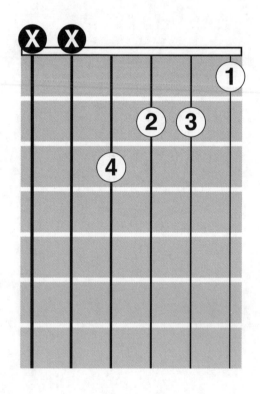

F°

F Diminished

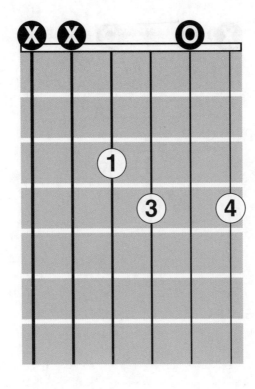

Fsus2

F Suspended 2nd

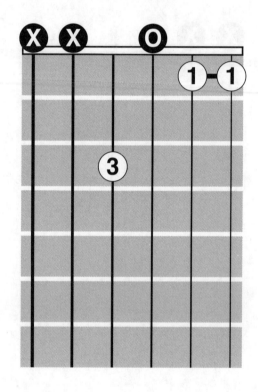

Fsus4

F Suspended 4th

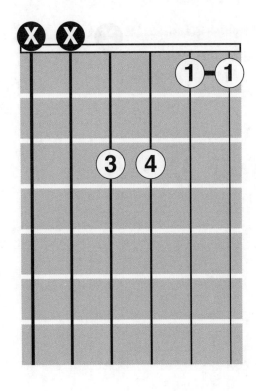

F5

F Power Chord

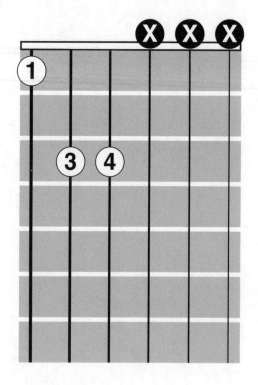

Fmaj6

F Major 6th

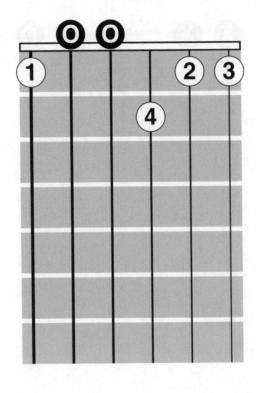

Fmaj7
F Major 7th

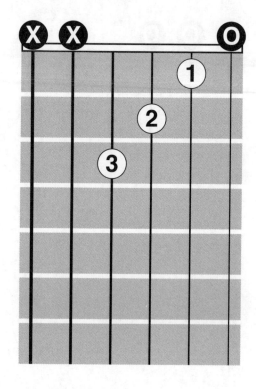

Fmaj7

F Major 7th
(alternative version)

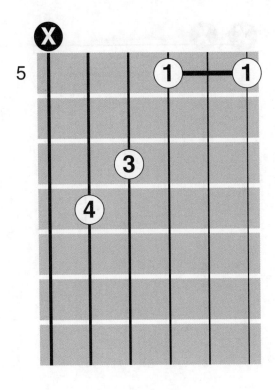

F7

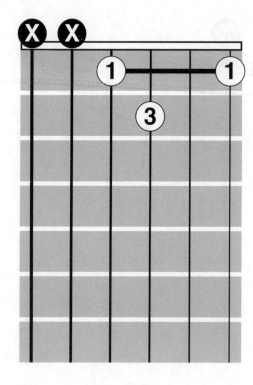

This will be named F7/E♭ in many songbooks.

Fm7

F Minor 7th
(barre chord)

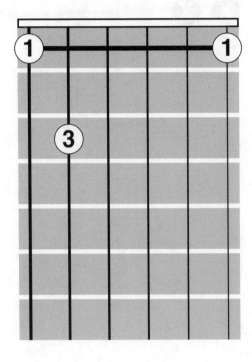

Fm7

F Minor 7th
(alternative version)

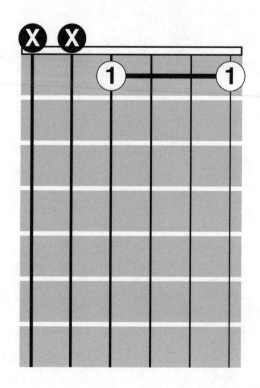

Fm/maj7

F Minor/Major 7th

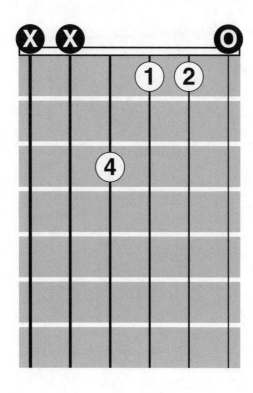

F°7

F Diminished 7th

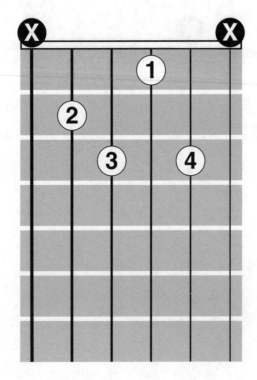

This is also known as B°7 and G#°7. The shape can be moved up by one fret to create A°7 (also known as D#°7 and E♭°7).

F9

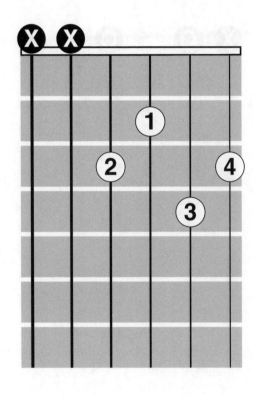

Fmaj9
F Major 9th

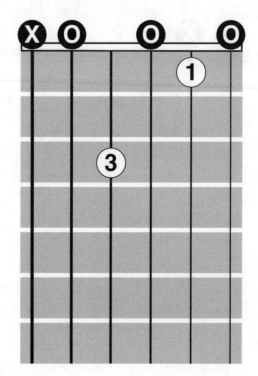

This will be named Fmaj9/A in many songbooks.

Fmaj9

F Major 9th
(alternative version)

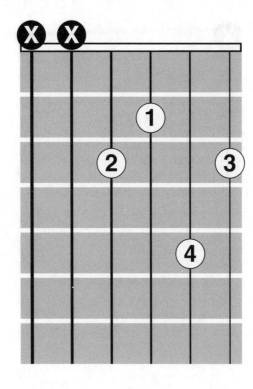

This will be named Fmaj9/A in many songbooks.

Fmaj9

F Major 9th
(alternative version)

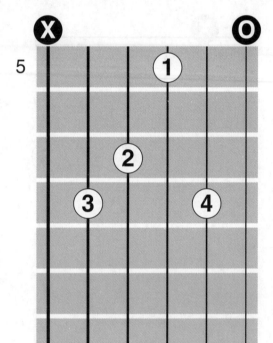

This will be named Fmaj9/A in many songbooks.

Fm9

F Minor 9th

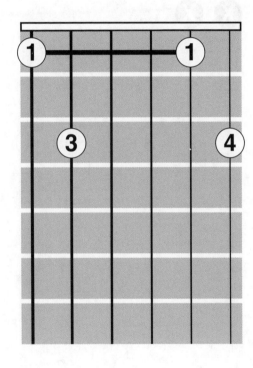

Fadd9

F Add 9th

C

C#/Db

D

D#/Eb

E

F

F#/Gb

G

G#/Ab

A

A#/Bb

B

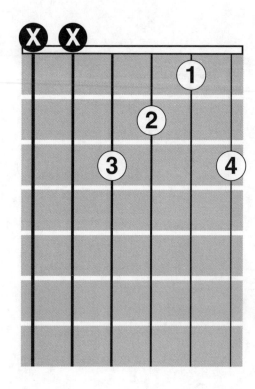

Fadd9

F Add 9th
(alternative version)

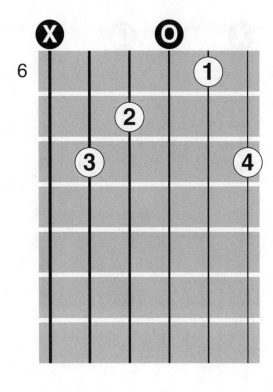

Fmadd9

F Minor Add 9th

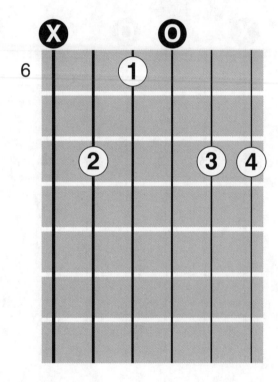

Fmaj7add11/A

F Major 7th Add 11/A

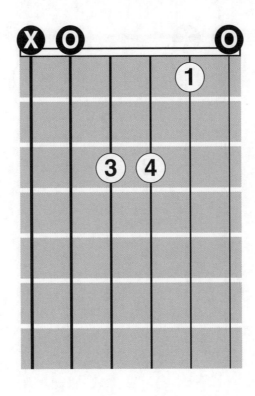

F#maj/Gbmaj

F# or Gb Major
(simplified version)

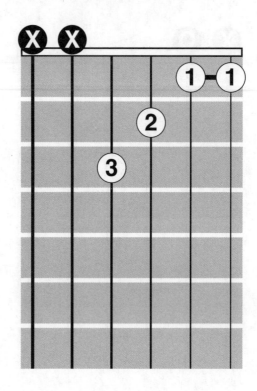

F#maj/G♭maj

F# or G♭ Major

(first inversion)

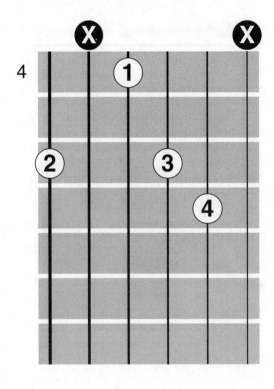

4

C

C#/D♭

D

D#/E♭

E

F

F#/G♭

G

G#/A♭

A

A#/B♭

B

F#maj/Gbmaj

F# or Gb Major
(barre chord)

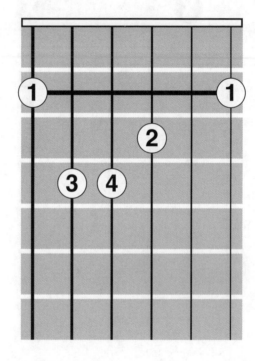

F#m/G♭m

F# or G♭ Minor
(simplified version)

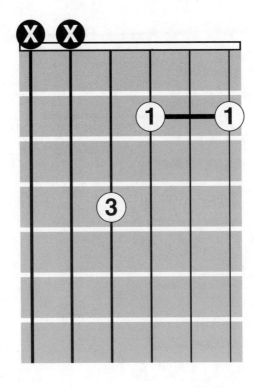

F#m/Gbm

F# or Gb Minor
(barre chord)

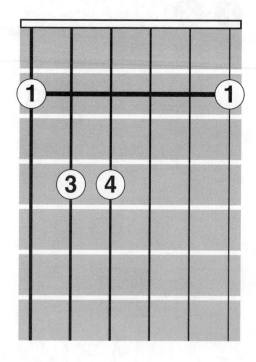

There aren't many bone-crushing heavy metal anthems
featuring F#m but then Led Zeppelin were not a typical
H.M. band. Their paean to the Norse gods of yore, 'Immigrant
Song', begins with a vocal cry to Thor over F#m before
crashing into a verse built on just A and E major.

F#+/G♭+

F# or G♭ Augmented

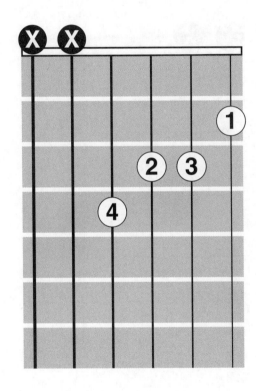

F#°/G♭°

F#/G♭ Diminished

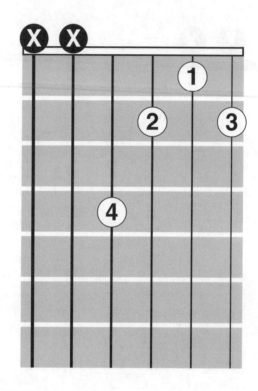

F#sus2/G♭sus2

F# or G♭ Suspended 2nd

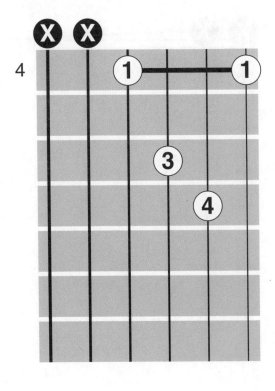

4

C

C#/D♭

D

D#/E♭

E

F

F#/G♭

G

G#/A♭

A

A#/B♭

B

F#sus4/G♭sus4

F# or G♭ Suspended 4th

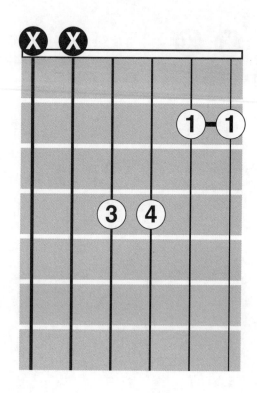

F#5/G♭5

F# or G♭ Power Chord

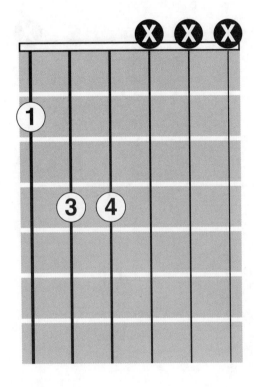

F#maj6/G♭maj6

F# or G♭ Major 6th

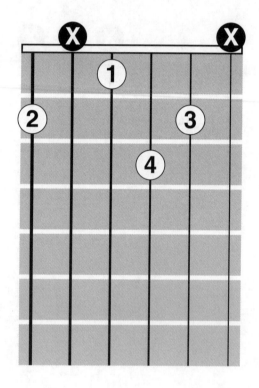

F#maj7/G♭maj7

F# or G♭ Major 7th

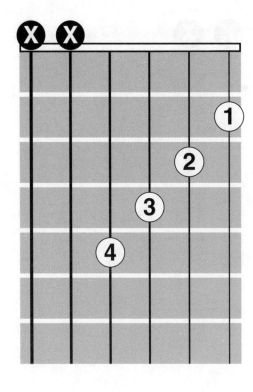

F#7/G♭7

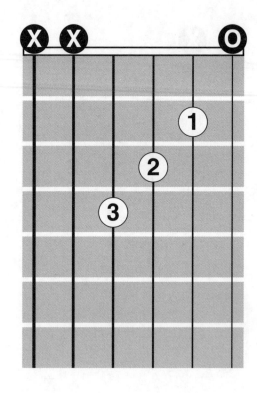

F#m7/G♭m7

F# or G♭ Minor 7th

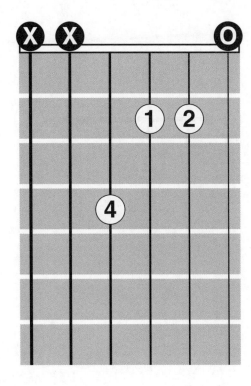

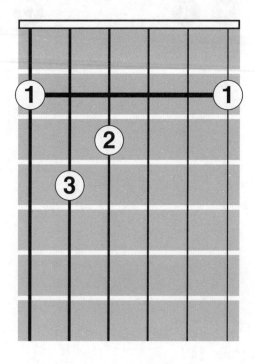

F#m/maj7/G♭m/maj7

F# or G♭ Minor/Major 7th
(barre chord)

F#°7/G♭°7

F# or G♭ Diminished 7th

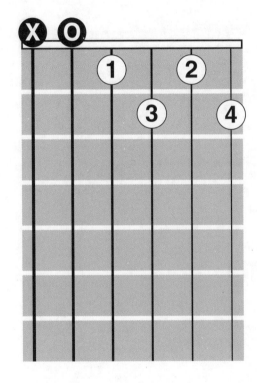

This chord is also known as E♭°7.

F#9/G♭9

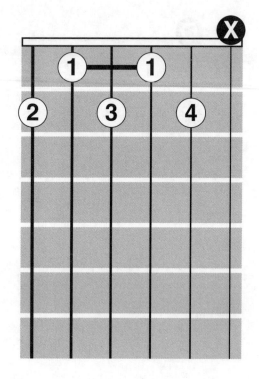

F#maj9/G♭maj9

F# or G♭ Major 9th

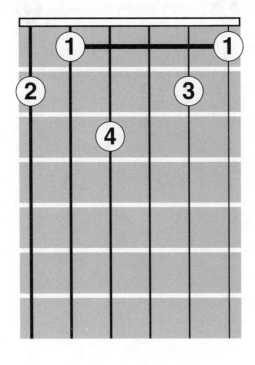

F#m9/G♭m9

F# or G♭ Minor 9th

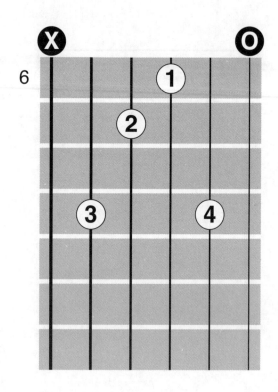

C
C#/D♭
D
D#/E♭
E
F
F#/G♭
G
G#/A♭
A
A#/B♭
B

F#add9/G♭add9

F# or G♭ Add 9th

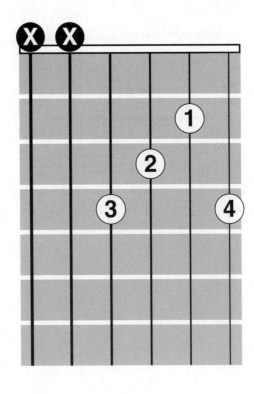

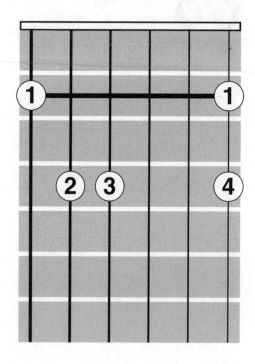

F#m add9/G♭m add9

F# or G♭ Minor Add 9th

(barre chord)

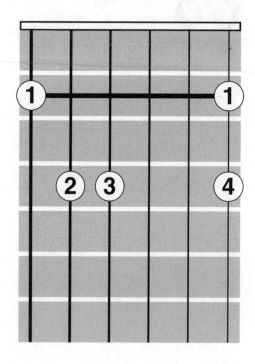

F#maj11/G♭maj11

F# or G♭ Major 11th

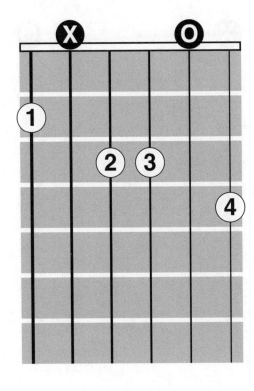

F#/G♭m7add11/C#

F# or G♭ Minor 7th Add 11/C#

C

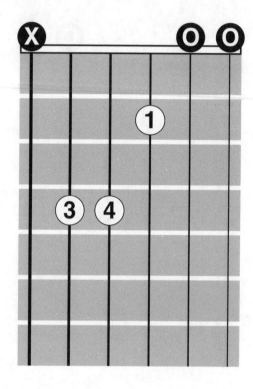

F#m11/G♭m11

F# or G♭ Minor 11th

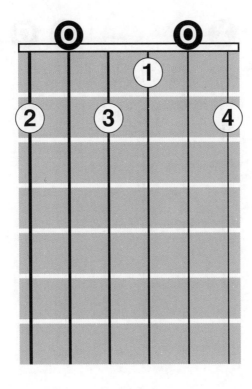

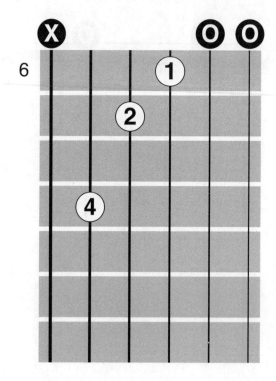

F#m11/G♭m11

F# or G♭ Minor 11th
(alternative version)

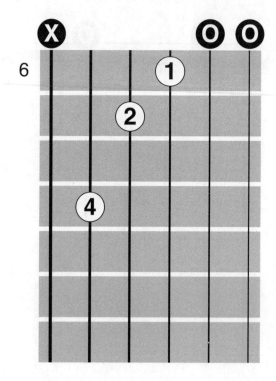

6

Gmaj

G Major
(basic version)

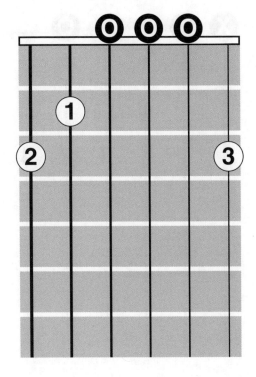

One of the most important chords to learn right from the start. There are few songs that do not feature G major somewhere so learn to play it cleanly and then practise smooth changes in a progression with C and D major. This will give you the three-chord trick in the key of G (the root of all early rock and roll).

C

C♯/D♭

D

D♯/E♭

E

F

F♯/G♭

G

G♯/A♭

A

A♯/B♭

B

Gmaj

G Major

(alternative version)

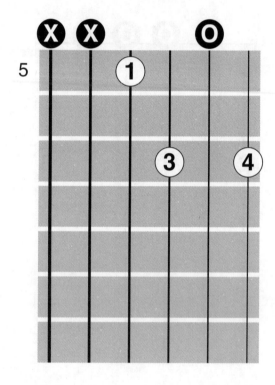

A useful alternative voicing higher up the fretboard producing a sparser, happier sound. Learn this chord and D7 and you will know the only chords needed to play Boney M's 'Brown Girl In The Ring'.

Gmaj

G Major
(first inversion)

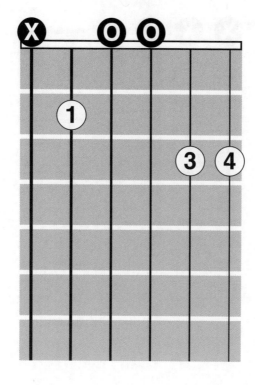

You will find this alternative shape listed in songbooks as G/B but it is an awkward alternative to the basic version on page 247 and rarely used.

Gmaj

G Major

(second inversion)

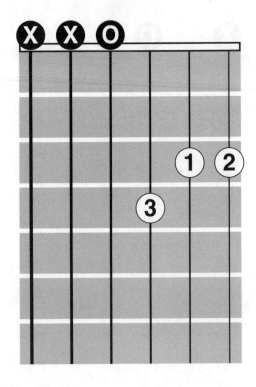

A useful variation if you need to move from F major to G quickly and smoothly as this is the basic Fmaj shape moved up two frets. Note that the third (not the second) finger is used at the fourth fret on the G string, as it naturally arches over to hold down the string and is therefore clear of the second string. Feel free to experiment with fingerings but remember that the conventional fingerings were chosen for a good reason!

Gmaj

G Major

(alternative second inversion)

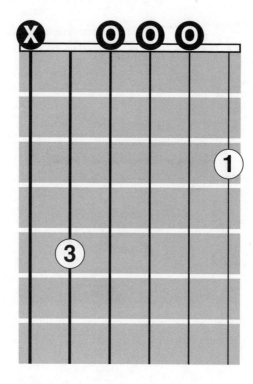

An alternative and more open-sounding voicing commonly listed in songbooks as G/D, but it should not be seen as a substitute for the basic G major triad on page 247.

Gmaj

G Major
(barre chord)

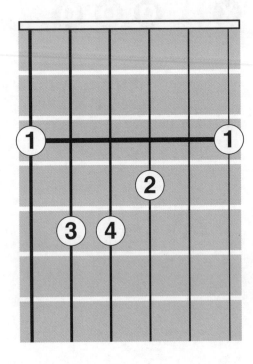

C

C#/Db

D

D#/Eb

E

F

F#/Gb

G

G#/Ab

A

A#/Bb

B

Gm

G Minor
(simplified version)

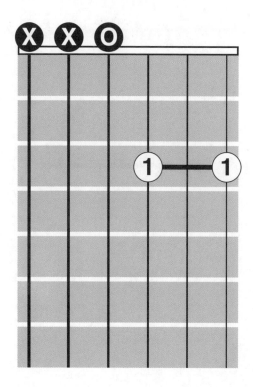

This is Gm second inversion and is easier to play than the first inversion. The barre chord version of Gm on page 254 serves as the basic version as it is easier to form, and this one-finger variation serves as the only alternative you will need.

C

C#/Db

D

D#/Eb

E

F

F#/Gb

G

G#/Ab

A

A#/Bb

B

Gm

G Minor
(barre chord)

C

C#/D♭

D

D#/E♭

E

F

F#/G♭

G

G#/A♭

A

A#/B♭

B

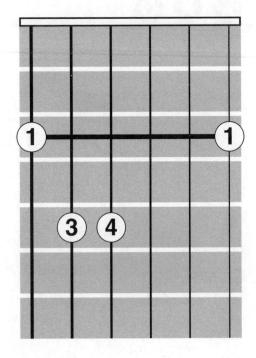

G+

G Augmented

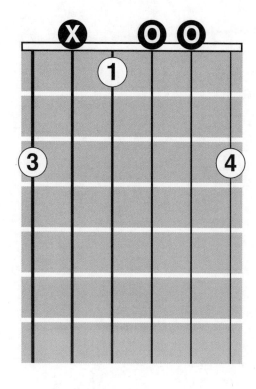

G°

G Diminished

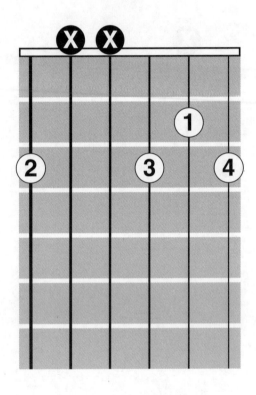

Gsus2

G Suspended 2nd

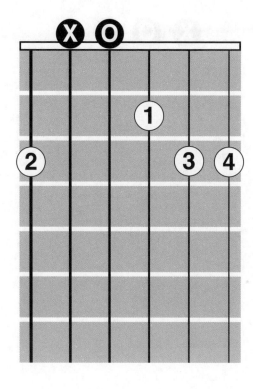

C

C♯/D♭

D

D♯/E♭

E

F

F♯/G♭

G

G♯/A♭

A

A♯/B♭

B

Gsus4

G Suspended 4th

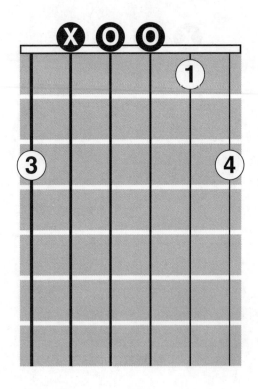

G5

G Power Chord

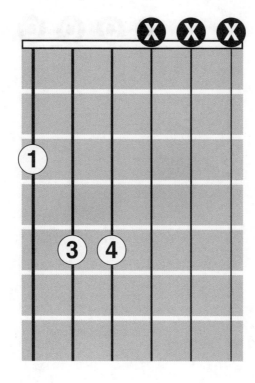

C

C#/Db

D

D#/Eb

E

F

F#/Gb

G

G#/Ab

A

A#/Bb

B

Gmaj6

G Major 6th

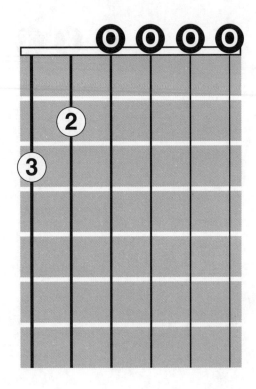

Gmaj7

G Major 7th

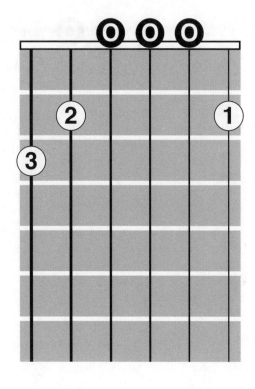

G7

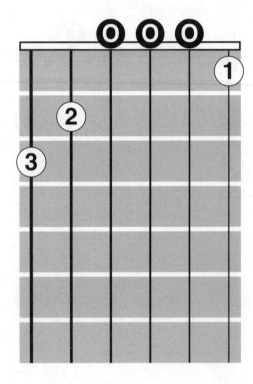

This chord can be simplified further by omitting the bottom two strings and only holding down the first finger on the first fret of the top E string.

C

C♯/D♭

D

D♯/E♭

E

F

F♯/G♭

G

G♯/A♭

A

A♯/B♭

B

Gm7

G Minor 7th
(barre chord)

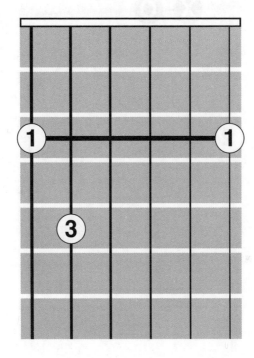

Hear this uncommon chord to best effect in the bridge of the title track of Black Sabbath's eponymous debut album where it is played against G major as Ozzy sings 'Oh God please help me'.

Gm/maj7

G Minor/Major 7th

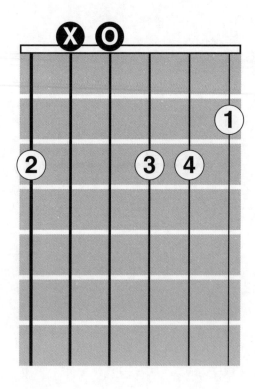

G°7

G Diminished 7th

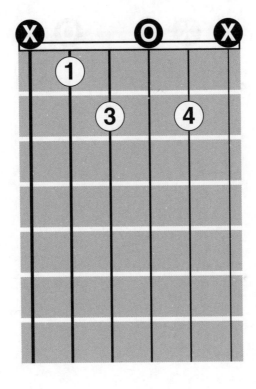

G9

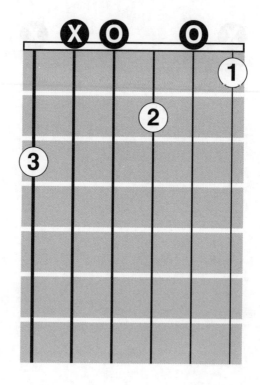

Gmaj9

G Major 9th

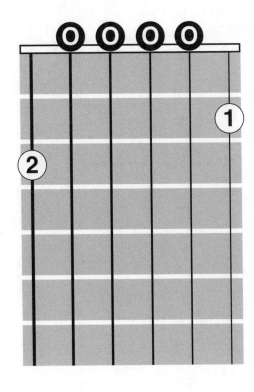

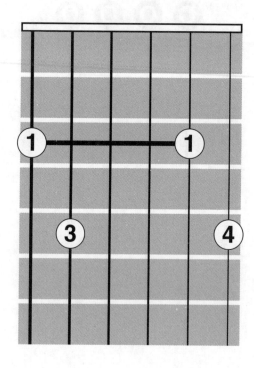

Gm9
G Minor 9th

Gadd9

G Add 9th

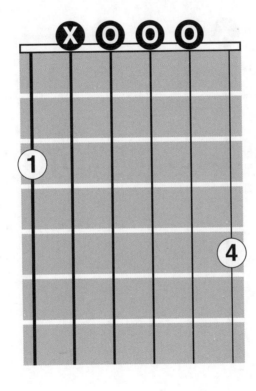

Gmadd9

G Minor Add 9th

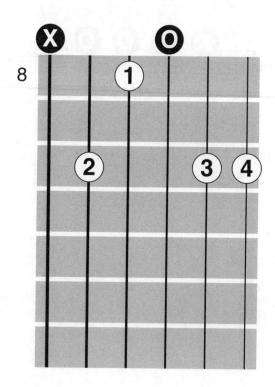

C

C#/Db

D

D#/Eb

E

F

F#/Gb

G

G#/Ab

A

A#/Bb

B

Gmaj7add11

G Major 7th Add 11

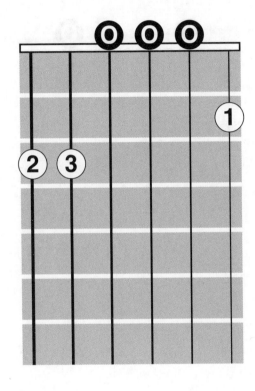

Gmaj11

G Major 11th

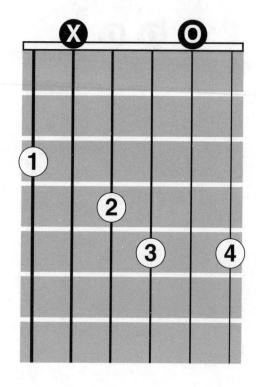

Gmaj11

G Major 11th
(alternative version)

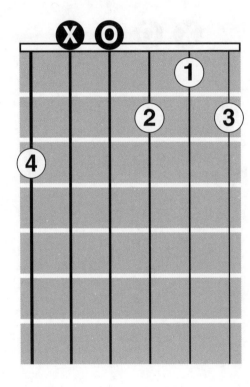

Gm7add11

G Minor 7th Add 11

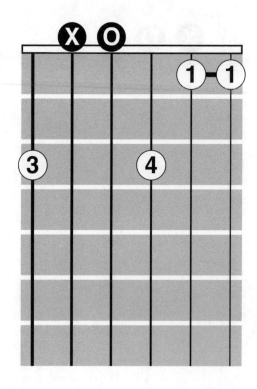

G♯maj/A♭maj

G♯ or A♭ Major
(simplified version)

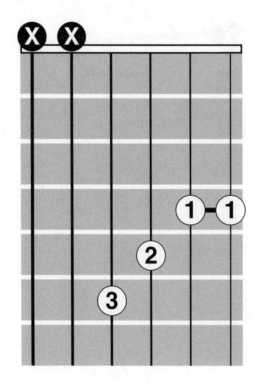

This is the F major shape moved up to the fourth fret.

G#maj/Abmaj

G# or Ab Major

(first inversion)

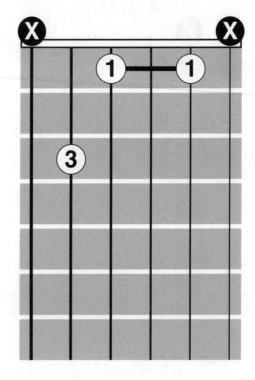

Known also as G# or Ab/C. The basic version of G#/Abmaj on the previous page is more practical and more common.

G♯maj/A♭maj

G♯ or A♭ Major
(second inversion)

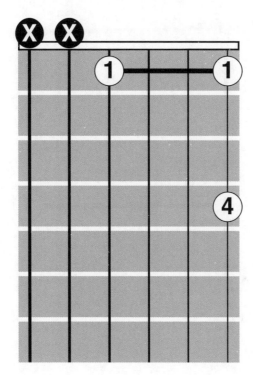

Known also as A♭/E♭. An awkward chord to finger if you have short fingers, but an easy stretch if you have larger hands and are keen to have every practical variation of the more common chords at your command.

G#maj/A♭maj

G# or A♭ Major

(barre chord)

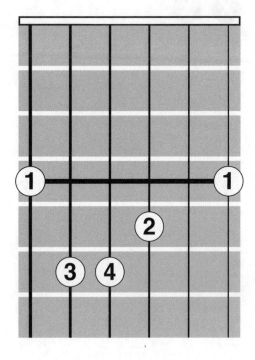

G#m/A♭m

G# or A♭ Minor
(simplified version)

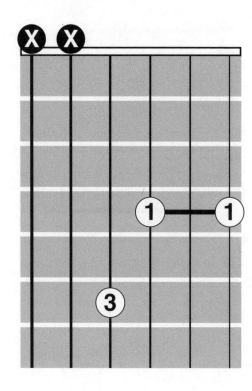

G♯m/A♭m

G♯ or A♭ Minor
(barre chord)

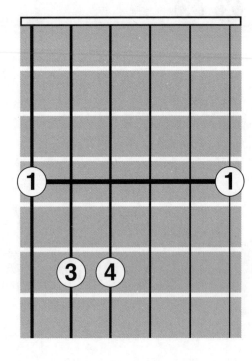

G#+/A♭+

G# or A♭ Augmented

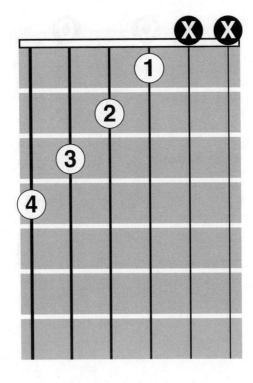

G#° or Ab°

G# or Ab Diminished

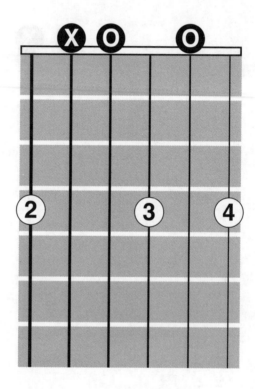

G♯sus2/A♭sus2

G♯ or A♭ Suspended 2nd

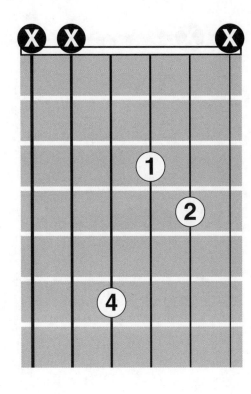

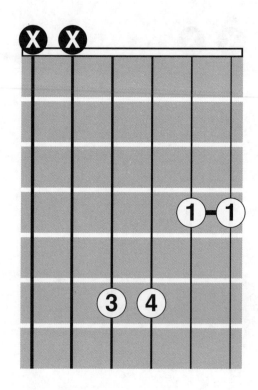

G#sus4/A♭sus4

G# or A♭ Suspended 4th

G#5/A♭5

G# or A♭ Power Chord

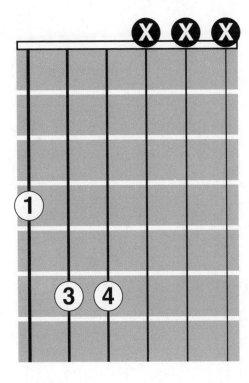

G#maj6/A♭maj6

G# or A♭ Major 6th

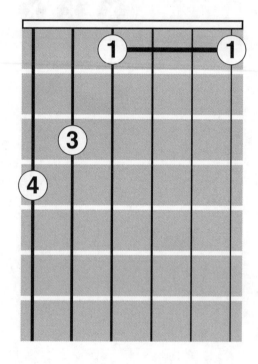

G#maj7/A♭maj7

G# or A♭ Major 7th
(barre chord)

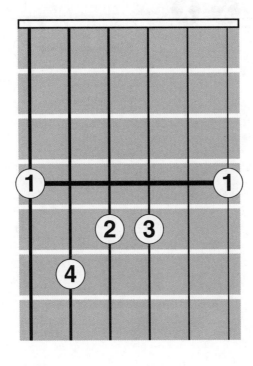

G#7/A♭7

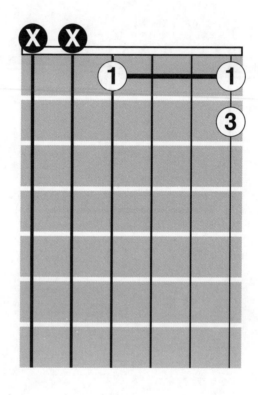

G♯m7/A♭m7

G♯ or A♭ Minor 7th
(barre chord)

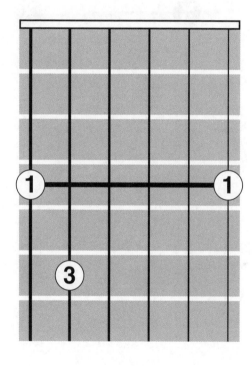

G#m/maj7/Abm/maj7

G# or Ab Minor/Major 7th

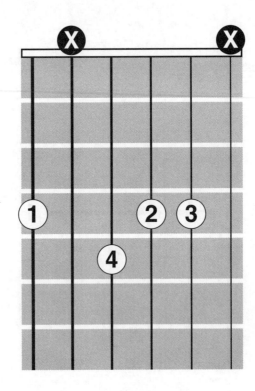

G#°7/A♭°7

G# or A♭ Diminished 7th

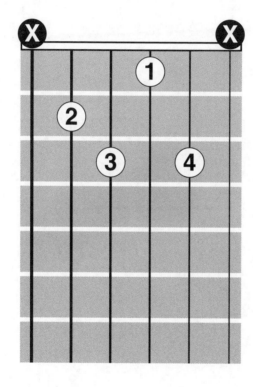

G#9 or A♭9

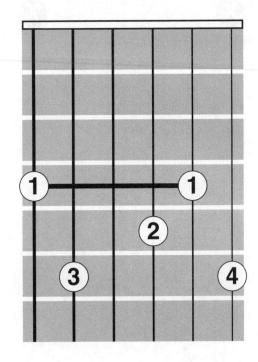

G♯m9/A♭m9

G♯ or A♭ Minor 9th

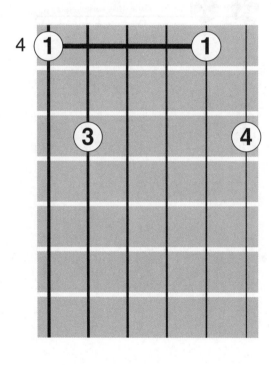

G#add9/A♭add9

G# or A♭ Add 9th

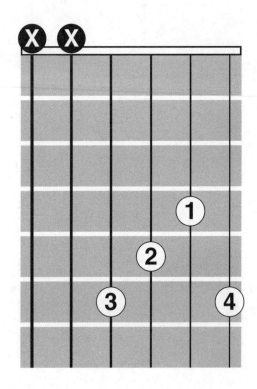

C

C#/D♭

D

D#/E♭

E

F

F#/G♭

G

G#/A♭

A

A#/B♭

B

G#m add9/A♭m add9

G# or A♭ Minor Add 9th

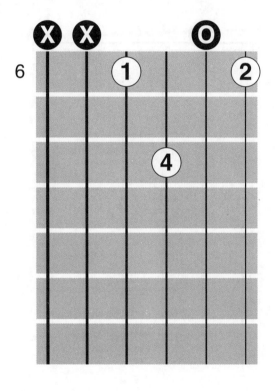

G#m7add11/Abm7add11

G# or Ab Minor 7th Add 11

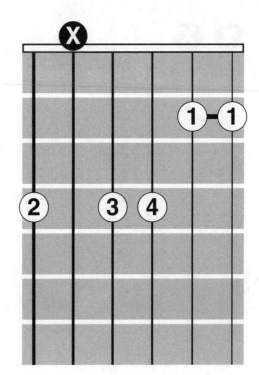

Amaj

A Major Triad
(basic version)

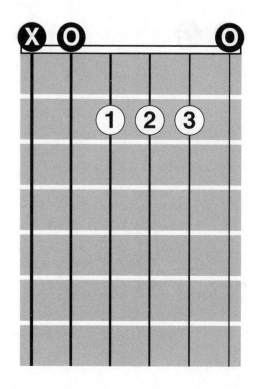

If you need to flesh out this light version add the open bottom E string. This will make a fuller version of A major known as its second inversion, named A/E in many songbooks. Blondie used only A, D and E major for their million-selling hit 'The Tide Is High'.

C

C#/Db

D

D#/Eb

E

F

F#/Gb

G

G#/Ab

A

A#/Bb

B

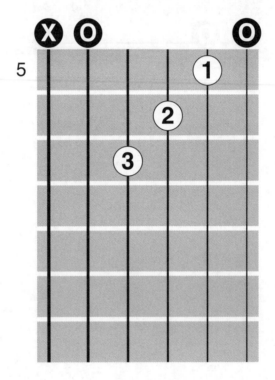

Amaj

A Major

(alternative version)

An alternative fingering further up the fretboard gives a
different voicing to A major, making it ideal for accompanying a
second guitarist who is playing the A major triad in its more
common form, on the second fret.

Amaj

A Major
(barre chord)

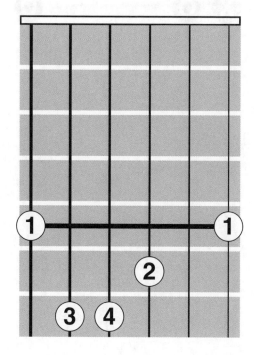

This is the only chord used in the verse of T. Rex's hit '20th-Century Boy'. The chorus adds B and E major.

Am

A Minor

(basic version)

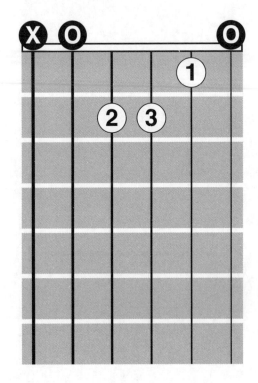

Queen's 'Who Wants To Live Forever' is the perfect example of how a few simple chords can create an emotive anthem. The verse starts on Am and adds Em, C, G, A and D major with just Cmaj, Gmaj and Am again in the chorus.

Am

A Minor
(half barred)

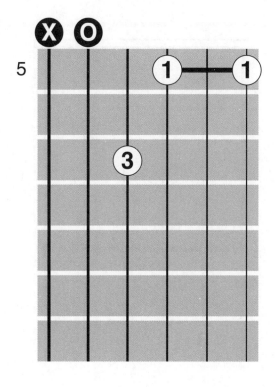

Am

A Minor
(barre chord)

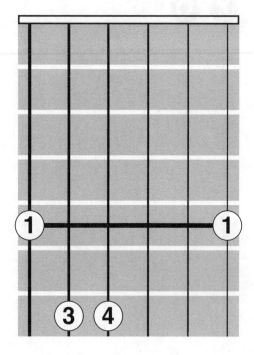

Jimi Hendrix took Bob Dylan's 'All Along The Watchtower' and made it something very special by playing with the simple three-chord structure of Am, G and F major. Compare Hendrix's reworking with Dylan's original to hear what can be achieved with three chords, brilliant technique and a bold approach to covering other artists' songs.

A+

A Augmented

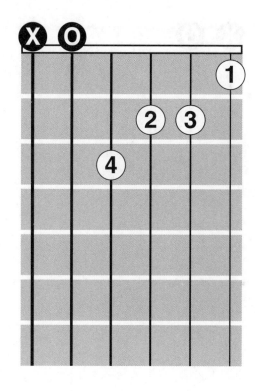

A°

A Diminished

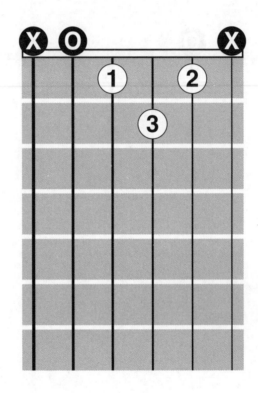

Asus2

A Suspended 2nd

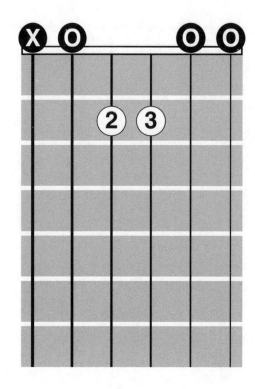

Asus4
A Suspended 4th

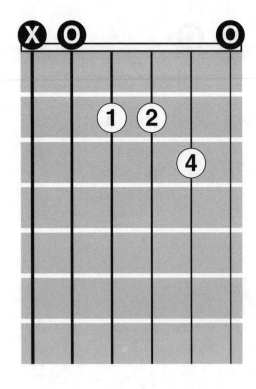

A5

A Power Chord

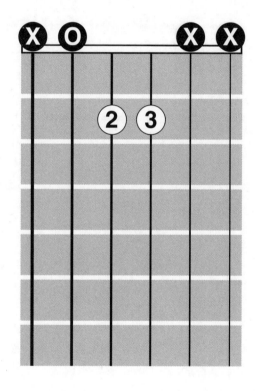

Amaj6

A Major 6th

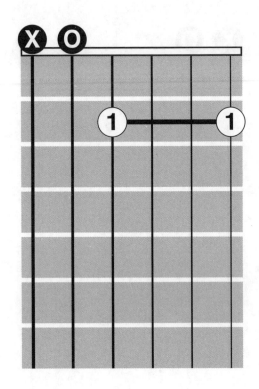

Amaj6

A Major 6th

(alternative version)

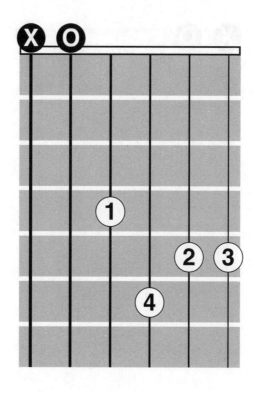

Amaj7

A Major 7th

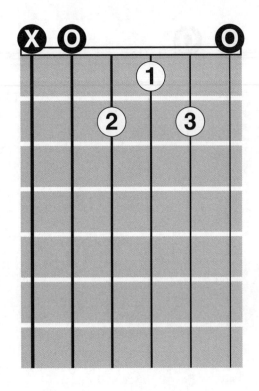

Amaj7

A Major 7th

(alternative version)

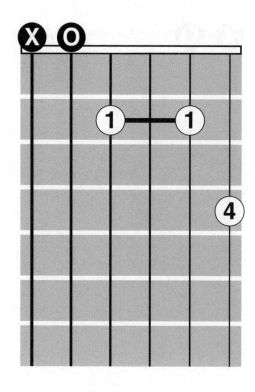

Amaj7
A Major 7th
(alternative version)

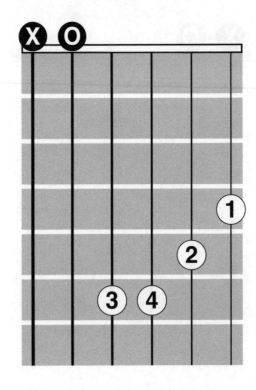

Amaj7

A Major 7th

(alternative version)

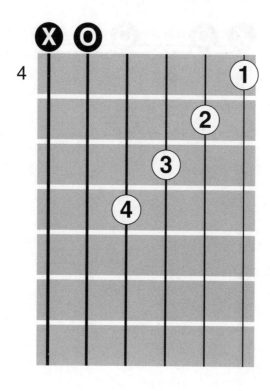

A7

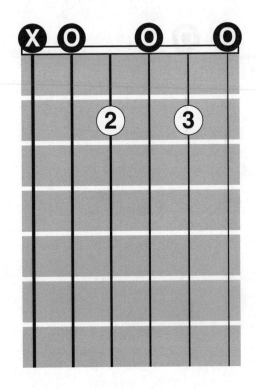

Am7

A Minor 7th

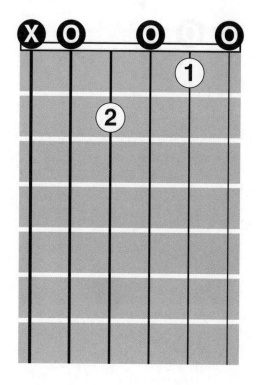

Hear how effective this chord can be as a transition in David Bowie's 'Space Oddity' where it smooths the change from Am to Dm in the last line of each verse ('take your protein pills and put your helmet on').

Am7

A Minor 7th
(alternative version)

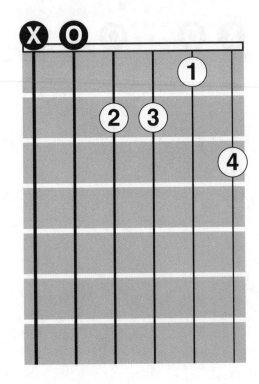

Am/maj7

A Minor/Major 7th

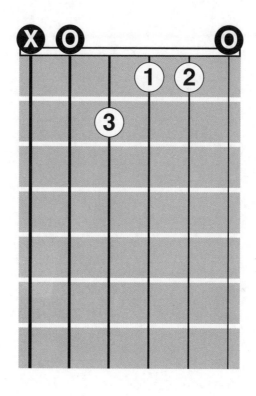

A°7

A Diminished 7th

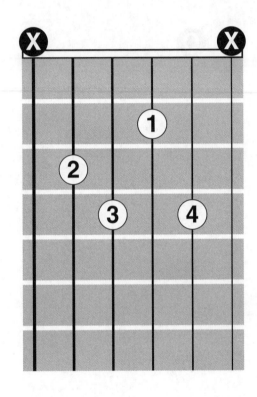

A9

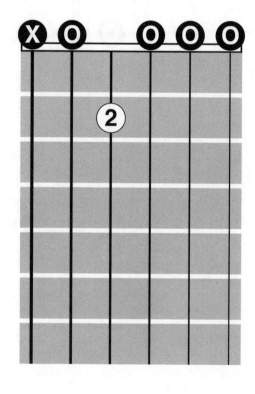

A9

(alternative version)

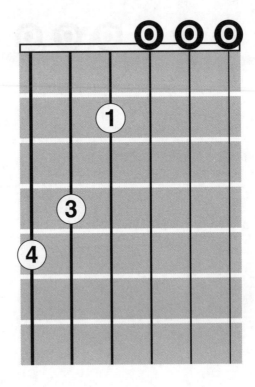

Amaj9

A Major 9th

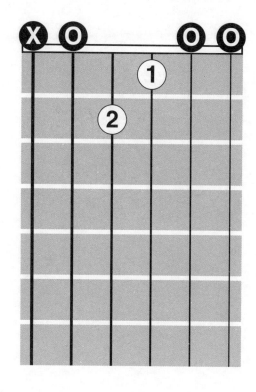

Amaj9

A Major 9th

(alternative version)

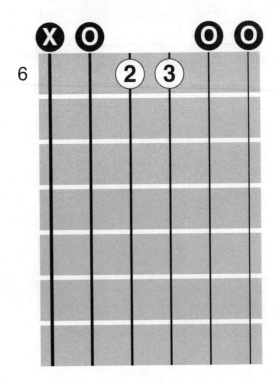

Aadd9

A Add 9th

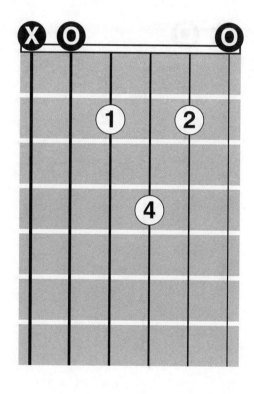

Aadd9

A Add 9th

(alternative version)

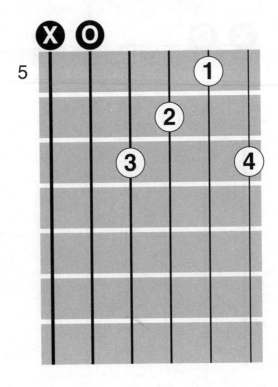

Aadd9

A Add 9th

(alternative version)

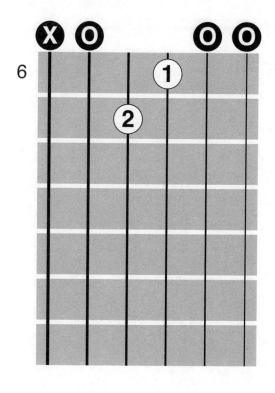

6

Am add9

A Minor Add 9th

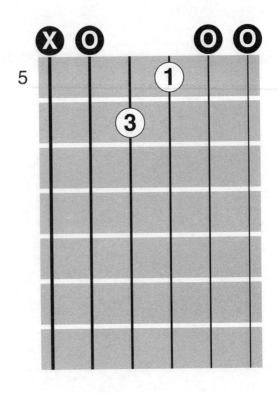

5

Amaj7add11

A Major 7th Add 11

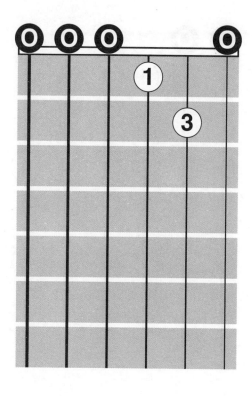

Amaj7add11/E

A Major 7th Add 11/E

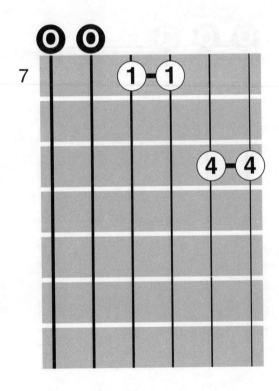

Amaj11
A Major 11th

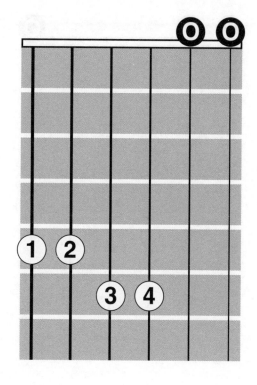

Am7add11

A Minor 7th Add 11

C

C#/Db

D

D#/Eb

E

F

F#/Gb

G

G#/Ab

A

A#/Bb

B

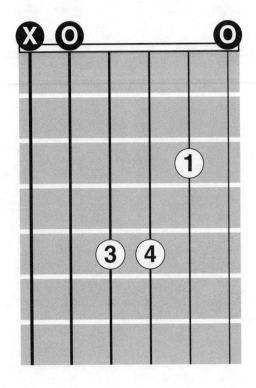

Am11

A Minor 11th

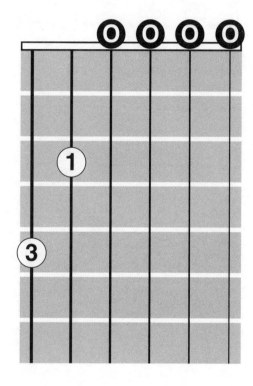

Am11

A Minor 11th

(alternative version)

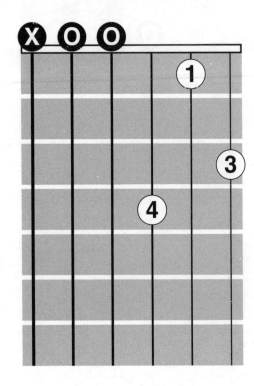

Am11

A Minor 11th
(alternative version)

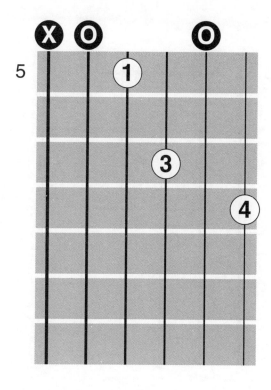

Am11

A Minor 11th

(alternative version)

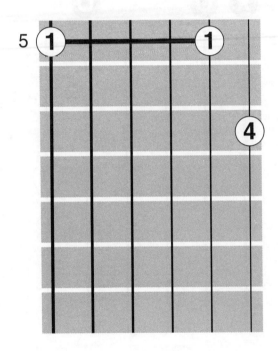

A#maj/B♭maj

A# or B♭ Major
(simplified version)

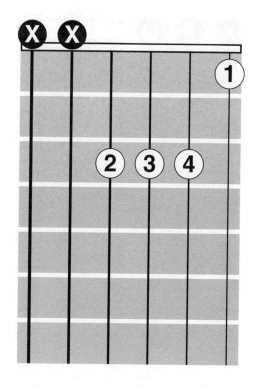

This is simply the basic Bmaj shape moved down one fret to produce B♭maj.

A#maj/Bbmaj

A# or Bb Major

(first inversion)

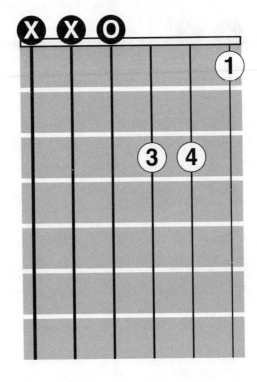

Although this is strictly the first inversion (Bb/D) it is also the simplest and easiest fingering for Bb major.

A♯maj/B♭maj

A♯ or B♭ Major
(alternative first inversion)

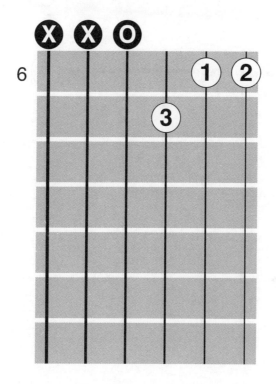

6

A simple shape higher up the neck gives a more suspenseful and spacious voicing than the chord on the previous page.

C

C♯/D♭

D

D♯/E♭

E

F

F♯/G♭

G

G♯/A♭

A

A♯/B♭

B

A#maj/Bbmaj

A# or Bb Major
(barre chord)

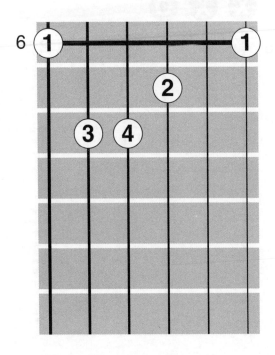

6

Hear how effective it can be to step down a semitone instead of a whole tone in 'The Man With The Child In His Eyes' by Kate Bush, when she moves from Bm to Bbmaj in the line 'Nobody knows about my man'. She composed on the piano so she would have found this progression more natural than it is on the guitar, but guitarists can pick up tips like this from keyboard players.

A♯m/B♭m

A♯ or B♭ Minor
(simplified version)

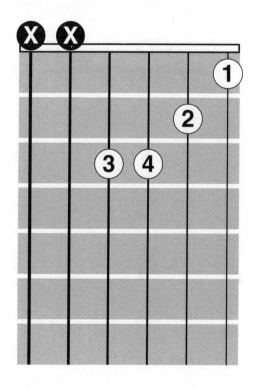

This chord will be named B♭m/F in many songbooks.

A#m/B♭m

A# or B♭ Minor
(barre chord)

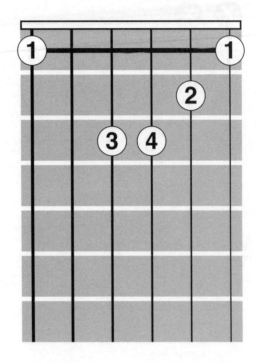

A#+/B♭+

A# or B♭ Augmented

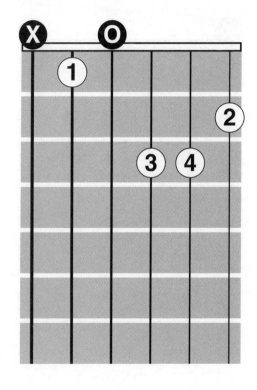

C
C#/Db
D
D#/Eb
E
F
F#/Gb
G
G#/Ab
A
A#/Bb
B

A#°/Bb°

A# or Bb Diminished

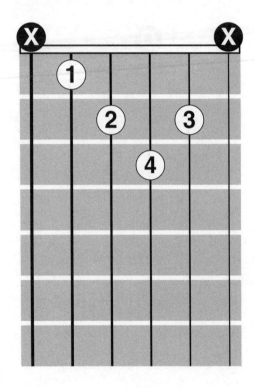

A♯sus2/B♭sus2

A♯ or B♭ Suspended 2nd

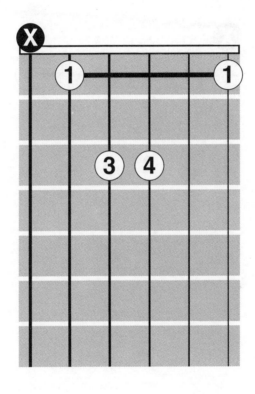

A#sus4/Bbsus4

A# or Bb Suspended 4th

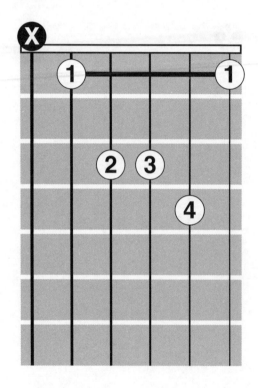

A♯5/B♭5

A♯ or B♭ Power Chord

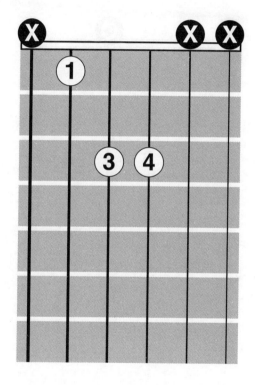

A#maj6/B♭maj6

A# or B♭ Major 6th

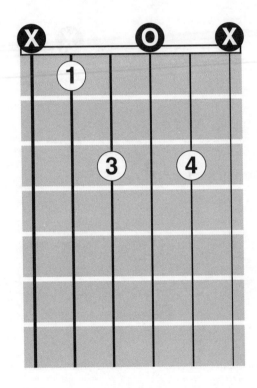

A#maj7/B♭maj7

A# or B♭ Major 7th

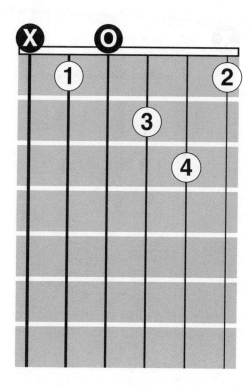

A#7/B♭7

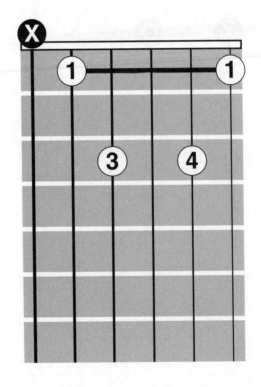

A♯m7/B♭m7

A♯ or B♭ Minor 7th

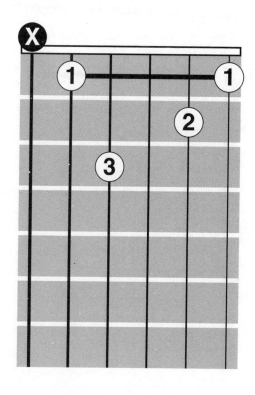

C

C♯/D♭

D

D♯/E♭

E

F

F♯/G♭

G

G♯/A♭

A

A♯/B♭

B

349

A#m/maj7/B♭m/maj7

A# or B♭ Minor/Major 7th
(barre chord)

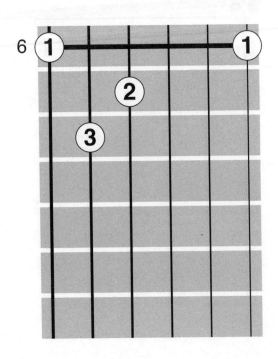

C
C#/D♭
D
D#/E♭
E
F
F#/G♭
G
G#/A♭
A
A#/B♭
B

A♯°7/B♭°7

A♯ or B♭ Diminished 7th

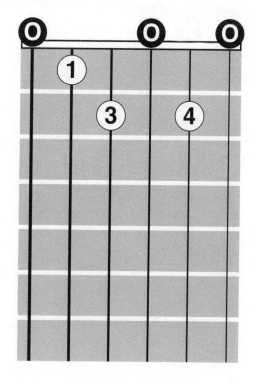

A#9/B♭9

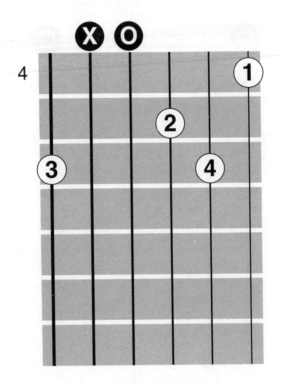

A♯maj9/B♭maj9

A♯ or B♭ Major 9th

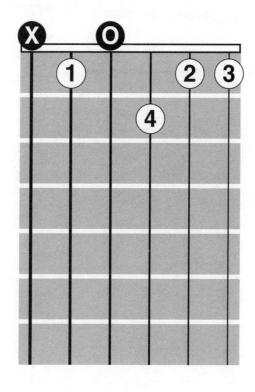

A#m9/Bbm9

A# or Bb Minor 9th

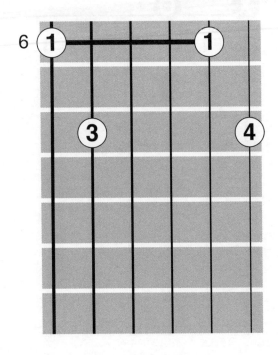

A#add9/B♭add9
A# or B♭ Add 9th

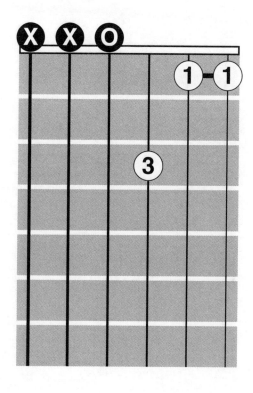

A#m add9/B♭m add9

A# or B♭ Minor Add 9th

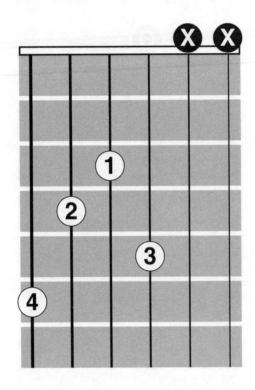

A♯maj11/B♭maj11

A♯ or B♭ Major 11th
(barre chord)

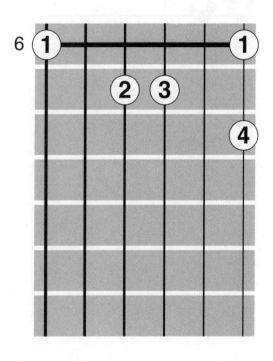

Bmaj

B Major
(basic version)

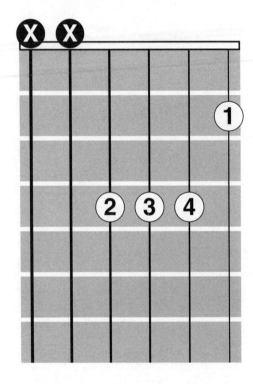

For this simplified barre chord the first finger holds down the second fret on the top E string instead of lying across all six strings at the second fret. This is the easiest version of B major and so it should be the first to be learnt, but technically it is B major second inversion and will be noted in many songbooks as B/F# to denote that F# is now the root and the top note. B major first inversion is too awkward for beginners.

Bmaj

B Major

(barre chord)

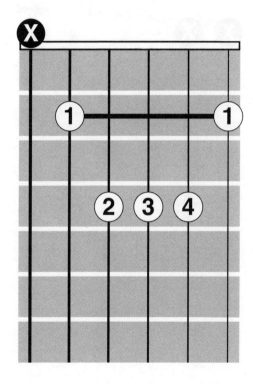

Add E and A major to B and you can play David Bowie's 'Jean Genie'.

Bm

B Minor

(basic version)

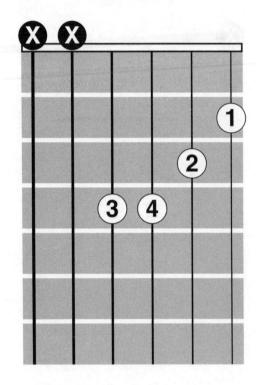

Bm

B Minor
(barre chord)

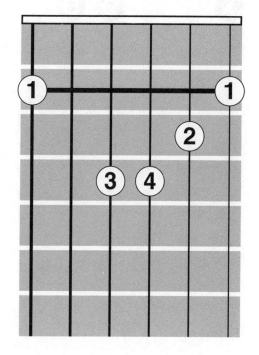

Hear how effective a major-to-minor progression can be in
The Who's 'Behind Blue Eyes' when this chord follows E major
in the line 'I have hours'. The other chords in the verses are C,
G, D and A major.

B+

B Augmented

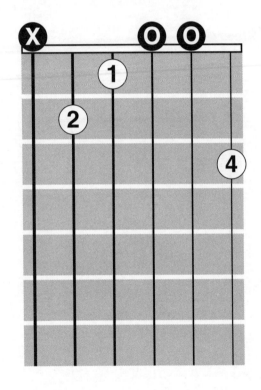

C

C#/Db

D

D#/Eb

E

F

F#/Gb

G

G#/Ab

A

A#/Bb

B

B°

B Diminished

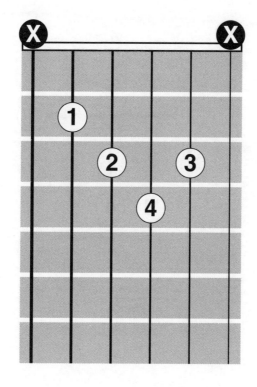

Bsus2

B Suspended 2nd

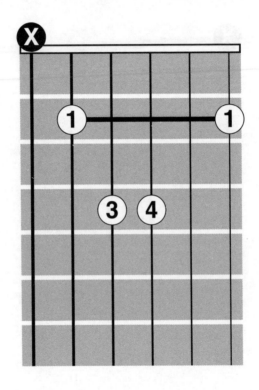

Bsus4

B Suspended 4th

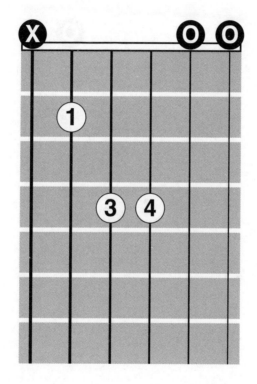

The strangeness of this chord is best appreciated by listening to indie Goth classic 'Bela Lugosi's Dead' by Bauhaus. The other chords in the song are A, B, C# and D major.

B5

B Power Chord

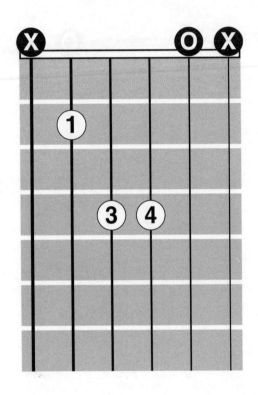

Bmaj6

B Major 6th

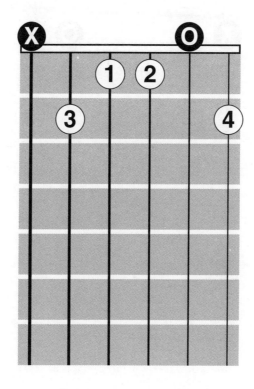

C

C#/Db

D

D#/Eb

E

F

F#/Gb

G

G#/Ab

A

A#/Bb

B

Bmaj7

B Major 7th

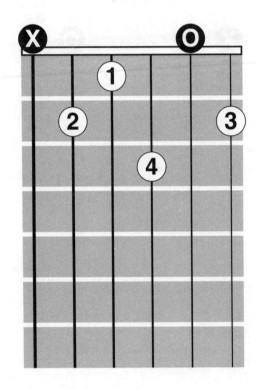

B7

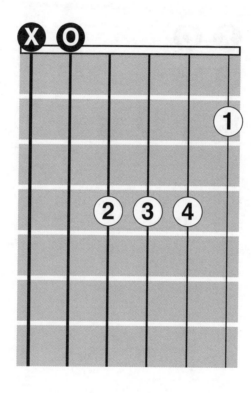

Bm7

B Minor 7th

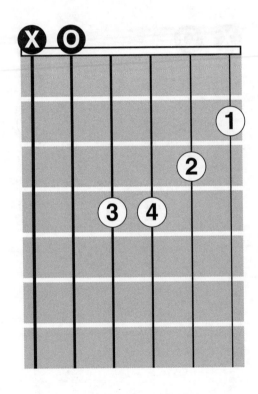

Bm/maj7

B Minor/Major 7th

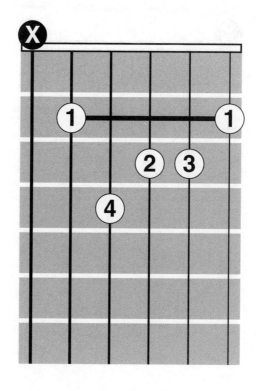

B°7

B Diminished 7th

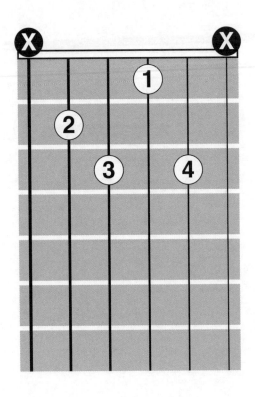

B9

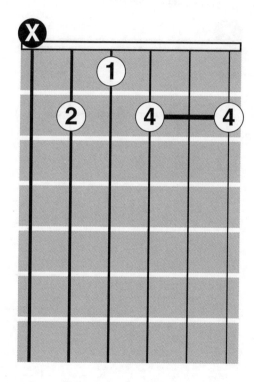

Hear the distinctive characteristic of this unusual chord in the Beach Boys' 'California Girls' in the first verse, accompanying the line 'I really dig those styles they wear'. The other chords in the verse are B, E and F# major. Chorus chords are Bmaj, C#m7, Amaj, Bm7, Gmaj and Am7.

Bmaj9

B Major 9th

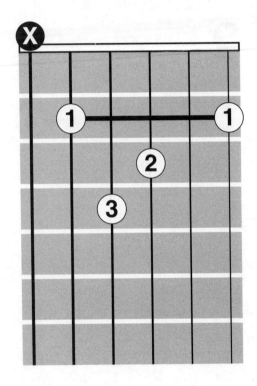

Bm9

B Minor 9th

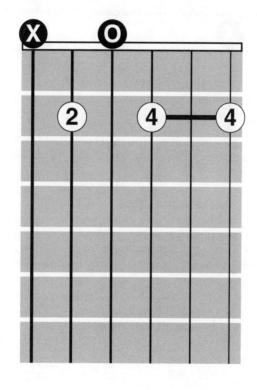

Badd9

B Add 9th

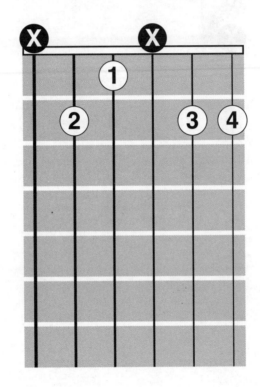

Bmadd9

B Minor Add 9th

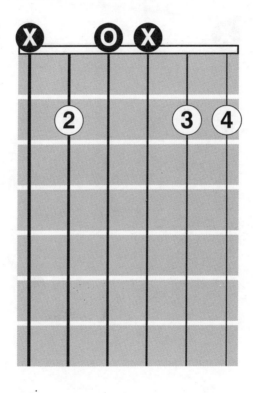

Bmaj11

B Major 11th

C

C♯/D♭

D

D♯/E♭

E

F

F♯/G♭

G

G♯/A♭

A

A♯/B♭

B

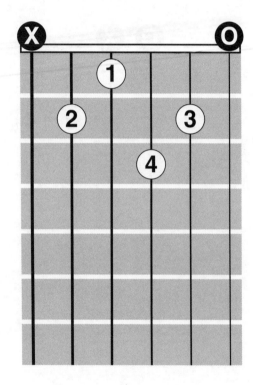

Bmaj11

B Major 11th

(alternative version)

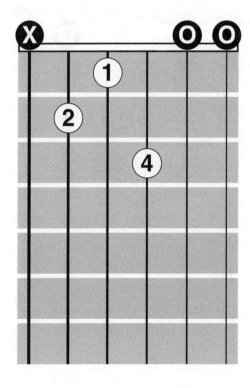

Bmaj11

B Major 11th
(alternative version)

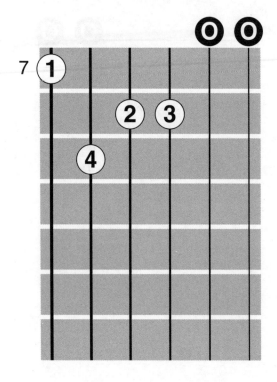

Bm7add11

B Minor 7th Add 11

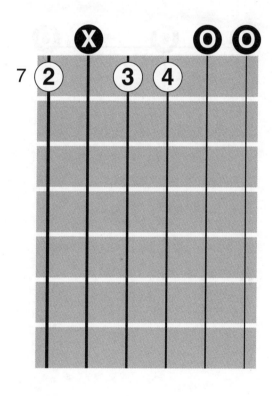

Bm11

B Minor 11th

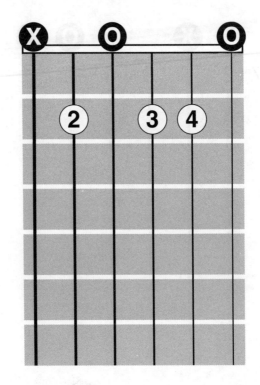

C

C#/Db

D

D#/Eb

E

F

F#/Gb

G

G#/Ab

A

A#/Bb

B

Bm11

B Minor 11th
(alternative version)

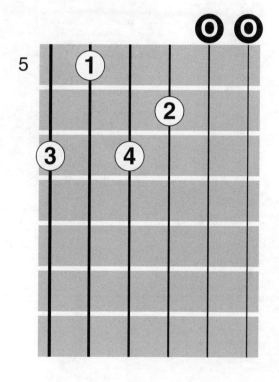